WINNING
WORDS

WINNING WORDS

Classic Quotes from the World of Sports

MICHAEL BENSON

TAYLOR TRADE PUBLISHING
Lanham • New York • Boulder • Toronto • Plymouth, UK

Published by Taylor Trade Publishing
An imprint of The Rowman & Littlefield Publishing Group, Inc.
4501 Forbes Boulevard, Suite 200, Lanham, Maryland 20706
www.rlpgtrade.com

Estover Road, Plymouth PL6 7PY, United Kingdom

Distributed by NATIONAL BOOK NETWORK

Library of Congress Cataloging-in-Publication Data

Benson, Michael.
 Winning words : classic quotes from the world of sports / Michael Benson.
     p. cm.
  ISBN-13: 978-1-58979-347-7 (cloth : alk. paper)
  ISBN-10: 1-58979-347-1 (cloth : alk. paper)
 1. Sports—Quotations, maxims, etc. I. Title.
 GV706.8.B46 2008
 798—dc22

                                                        2008009983

Acknowledgments

THE AUTHOR would like to thank the following individuals without whose assistance the compilation of these quotes would have been impossible: Eddie Behringer, Tekla and Matthew Benson, Keith Brenner, Peter Burford, Anne Darrigan, Jake Elwell, Scott Frommer, Lisa M. Grasso, Mark Harris, Thom Loverro, Jim Raleigh, and Carl Soloway.

INTRODUCTION

WHAT DOES IT TAKE to inspire a team to work together and win? That's the question this book sets out to answer. It is the infusion of confidence, the teaching of a system and philosophy, the massaging of the ego, and the simultaneous development of group ego—the sense that the team is bigger than the individual. It is wisdom and humor. It is adaptability, for what inspires two teammates may be two completely different things—and what inspires the group as a whole may be a third.

In this book you'll find almost one thousand of the world's most inspirational quotes, pep talks, and solid advice on how to get up off your butt and get out and win—no matter what game you're playing.

In some cases explanatory notes will be attached to the quotes, to help put their meaning in context. This was not done without solid consideration; after all, it is best to let the words pack their own punch. But there are some quotes that simply cannot be appreciated unless you have at least a factoid or two of background. Often the context has to do with mortality. Lou Gehrig's farewell speech comes to mind.

Other times it has to do with overcoming obstacles. It is important to understand, for example, why it was more inspirational for Jim Abbott to throw a no-hitter than it was when Nolan Ryan threw one. So, if you are a sports fanatic, sorry. The idea is to inspire anyone who wants to read this, regardless of his or her sports knowledge.

Also, sprinkled throughout will be short biographies of the coaches and athletes whose words are gathered here.

The quotes are organized into fairly flexible categories. Within those categories, entries are arranged alphabetically by the name of the person being quoted.

So, here's to the hope that you'll find at least one quote on these pages that'll give you the boost you need to attain your own personal victory.

ABILITY

"Natural abilities are like natural plants; they need pruning by study."

—Red Auerbach, basketball

"It is a fine thing to have ability, but the ability to discover ability in others is the true test."

—Lou Holtz, football

"Ability is a poor man's wealth."

—John Wooden, basketball

ACCOMPLISHMENTS

"A lot of guys go through their whole careers and don't win a championship, but are still great coaches."

—Chuck Daly, basketball

"If everything had already been done, there would be nothing left for young people to accomplish. There are always going to be people who run faster, jump higher, dive deeper, and come up drier."

—Darrell Royal, football

ADULTHOOD

"Baseball was made for kids, and grown-ups only screw it up."

—Bob Lemon, baseball

ADVERSITY

"You never know how a horse will pull until you hook him up to a heavy load."

—Paul "Bear" Bryant, football

"I didn't just jump back on the bike and win. There were a lot of ups and downs, good results and bad results, but this time I didn't let the lows get to me."

—Lance Armstrong, bicycle racing

"Doctors and scientists said that breaking the four-minute mile was impossible, that one would die in the attempt. Thus, when I got up from the track after collapsing at the finish line, I figured I was dead."

—Roger Bannister, track and field

"In adversity there is opportunity. Show me someone who has done something worthwhile, and I'll show you someone who has overcome adversity. I've never known anybody to achieve anything without overcoming adversity. Adversity is another way to measure the greatness of individuals. I never had a crisis that didn't make me stronger."

—Lou Holtz, football

"I've seen very little character in players who never had to face adversity."

—Tom Landry, football

"Adversity is an opportunity for heroism."

—Marv Levy, football

"When you are playing against a stacked deck, compete even harder. Show the world how much you'll fight for the winner's circle. If you do, someday the cellophane will crackle off a fresh pack, one that belongs to you, and the cards will be stacked in your favor."

—Pat Riley, basketball

"Even in the most impossible situations, stand tall, keep our heads up, shoulders back, keep moving, running, looking up, demonstrating our pride, dignity, and defiance."

—Bill Walsh, football

"You can't get much done in life if you only work on the days when you feel good."

—Jerry West, basketball

"Adversity is the state in which man most easily becomes acquainted with himself, being especially free of admirers then."

—John Wooden, basketball

AGE

"The age factor means nothing to me. I'm old enough to know my limitations and I'm young enough to exceed them.

JOHN WOODEN

If you had to guide your life using the words of one man in sports, John Wooden might be your best bet. He was the coach of the UCLA Bruins basketball team for 27 seasons and was at the helm during the longest and greatest dynasty in college athletics history. His words of wisdom are scattered throughout this book. Wooden was born in Martinsville, Indiana, on October 14, 1910. As a schoolboy, Wooden led Martinsville High to the Indiana State Championships three straight years. He went to Purdue where he played basketball and baseball. But it was on the court that he excelled, winning All-America honors three times, from 1930–1932. In 1932, Purdue won the national championship. After graduation he married his wife Nell, and began his coaching career at Dayton High School in Kentucky and then South Bend Central High School in Indiana. He served as a lieutenant in the navy during World War II. After the war, Wooden became athletic director at Indiana State University, his last job before becoming UCLA basketball coach. Today, he is 97 and remains college basketball's most prolific winner of NCAA championships, with ten. Of those ten titles, eight came consecutively, from 1966–1973. His career record was 865-203 (620-147 at UCLA). In UCLA's home arena, Pauley Pavilion, Wooden's teams won 149 games and lost two. At one point his team won 38 straight NCAA tournament games. He is the only person to be inducted into the National Basketball Hall of Fame both as a player and a coach. Wooden's wife, Nell, died in Los Angeles on March 21, 1985. They were married for 53 years. They had a son, James Hugh, and a daughter, Nancy Anne. Today John has seven grandchildren and 11 great-grandchildren.

I'm an 80-year-old rookie. And looking forward to it with boundless enthusiasm."

—Marv Levy, football

"I throw the ball as hard as ever, but it just takes longer to get to the plate."

—Don Newcombe, baseball

"Age is a case of mind over matter. If you don't mind, it don't matter. How old would you be if you didn't know how old you are?"

—Leroy "Satchel" Paige, baseball

AGGRESSIVENESS

"You're born with two strikes against you, so don't take a third one on your own."

—Connie Mack, baseball

ANGER

"Don't matter what they throw at us. Only angry people win football games."

—Darrell Royal, football

ATTENTION TO DETAIL

"In the successful organization, no detail is too small to escape close attention."

—Lou Holtz, football

"Inches make a champion."

—Vince Lombardi, football

"It's the little details that are vital. Little things make big things happen."

—John Wooden, basketball

ATTITUDE

"Football isn't necessarily won by the best players. It's won by the team with the best attitude."

—George Allen, football

"Life is precious. You should make everyone you meet or see happy."

—Sparky Anderson, baseball

"The ideal attitude is to be physically loose and mentally tight."

—Arthur Ashe, tennis

"If you want to be a champion, you've got to feel like one, you've got to act like one, you've got to look like one."

—Red Auerbach, basketball

"You can't control the weather, but you can control the atmosphere."

—Edward C. Behringer, horse racing

"A winner never whines."

—Paul Brown, football

"I think the most important thing of all for any team is a winning attitude. The coaches must have it. The players must have it. The student body must have it. If you have dedicated players who believe in themselves, you don't need a lot of talent."

—Paul "Bear" Bryant, football

"Nothing is work unless you'd rather be doing something else."

—George Halas, football

"Ability is what you are capable of doing. Motivation determines what you do. Attitude determines how well you do it."

—Lou Holtz, football

"Like life, basketball is messy and unpredictable. It has its way with you, no matter how hard you try to control it. The trick is to experience each moment with a clear mind and open heart. When you do that, the game—and life—will take care of itself."

—Phil Jackson, basketball

"Any guy who can maintain a positive attitude without much playing time certainly earns my respect."

—Earvin "Magic" Johnson, basketball

"You are never going to be driven anywhere worthwhile, but you sure as hell drive yourself to a lot of great places. It is up to you to drive yourself there."

—Bobby Knight, basketball

"Never let your head hang down. Never give up and sit down and grieve. Find another way. And don't pray when it rains if you don't pray when the sun shines."

—Leroy "Satchel" Paige, baseball

"Work like you don't need the money. Love like you've never been hurt. Dance like nobody's watching."

—Leroy "Satchel" Paige, baseball

"Believe deep down in your heart that you're destined to do great things. Besides pride, loyalty, discipline, heart, and mind, confidence is the key to all the locks."

—Joe Paterno, football

"Great effort springs naturally from a great attitude. If you have a positive attitude and constantly strive to give your best effort, eventually you will overcome your immediate problems and find you are ready for greater challenges."

—Pat Riley, basketball

JOE PATERNO

Joe Paterno has been the head coach of the Penn State football team since 1966. He has coached the Nittany Lions to five undefeated campaigns, and four times been named "Coach of the Year" by the American Football Coaches Association. At Penn State, Paterno is a wise and paternal figure with a reputation of absolute integrity. *Sports Illustrated* writer Rick Reilly once wrote, "In an era of college football in which it seems everybody's hand is either in the till or balled up in a fist, Paterno sticks out like a clean thumb."

"I've always believed that you can think positive just as well as you can think negative."

—Sugar Ray Robinson, boxing

"I became an optimist when I discovered that I wasn't going to win any more games by being anything else."

—Earl Weaver, baseball

AWARDS

"I've had Coach of the Year honors. I could care less about them. It doesn't mean a thing to me. My fun is winning a game. Being national champion is like the heavyweight crown. Coach of the Year and that stuff does not turn me on. If I had to choose between winning the conference and winning an honor, it wouldn't even be close."

—Bobby Bowden, football

AWARENESS

"I always know what's happening on the court. I see a situation occur, and I respond."

—Larry Bird, basketball

BAD HABIT

"You need to play with supreme confidence, or else you'll lose again, and then losing becomes a habit."

—Joe Paterno, football

BEGINNINGS

"I try to see each new season as a new challenge because I have a new team to work with, new opponents to encounter, and often new ideas and theories to try."

—Mike Krzyzewski, basketball

CHALLENGES

"There are millions of people out there ignoring disabilities and accomplishing incredible feats. I learned you can learn to do things differently, but do them just as well. I've learned that it's not the disability that defines you, it's how you deal with the challenges the disability presents you with. And I've learned that we have an obligation to the abilities we *do* have, not the disability."

—Jim Abbott, baseball

"One of the reasons I coach is because of the challenges. I want to meet the challenges and get a group of people to be successful in facing those challenges."

—Mike Krzyzewski, basketball

"I love the game. It's fun to play, period. I love running around and getting sweaty. I love trying to lead my team. I love facing the challenge of another team that's better."

—Jamila Wideman, basketball

CHAMPIONS

"Champions aren't made in the gyms. Champions are made from something they have deep inside them—a desire, a dream, a vision."

—Muhammad Ali, boxing

"The hard work starts when you become a champion. Everyone wants a shot at you, and every fight will be tougher than it would have been if you were just another contender."

—Eddie Futch, boxing

"Everybody on a championship team doesn't get publicity, but everyone can say he's a champion."

—Earvin "Magic" Johnson, basketball

"Champions take responsibility. When the ball is coming over the net, you can be sure I want the ball."

—Billie Jean King, tennis

"The only yardstick for success our society has is being a champion. No one remembers anything else."

—John Madden, football

"There's always the motivation of wanting to win. Everybody has that. But a champion needs, in his attitude, a motivation above and beyond winning."

—Pat Riley, basketball

"The mark of a true champion is to always perform near your own level of competency."

—John Wooden, basketball

CHANGE

"One thing that could be a problem is breaking old habits. It's not that you don't understand what the new responsibilities or plays are, but just the fact that you've been doing something a long time and you're kind of used to doing it, it's a habit, and that's not what's required in the other system and that means kind of undoing something before you can even start to do something new."

—Bill Belichick, football

"You must *be* the change you wish to see in the world."

—Mahatma Gandhi, political and spiritual leader

"You never stay the same. You either get better or you get worse."

—Jon Gruden, football

"Some people change, and some people change too late, and then you have a problem. Like the one we had back home in Newcomerstown when they had to give up driver's ed in the high school because the horse died."

—Woody Hayes, football

BILL BELICHICK

Bill Belichick grew up in a football family. His father played fullback for the Detroit Lions and coached for 33 years at the U.S. Naval Academy. Since 2000 Bill has been the head coach of the New England Patriots where he became the only coach in NFL history to win three Super Bowls in a four-year span.

One of the reasons for Belichick's success is his ability to get his team ready against the toughest competition and for the biggest games. His teams also tend to continue winning even when stricken with key injuries, a sign that the coach is just as important as the personnel when it comes to success.

Before coaching the Pats, Belichick spent five seasons as head coach of the Cleveland Browns and three with the New York Jets. His NFL coaching career began in 1975, at the age of 23, when he became assistant coach for the then-Baltimore Colts. One-year stints as assistant coach for the Lions and Broncos followed.

In 1979 Belichick began 12 years as a defensive assistant and special teams coach for the New York Giants. During that time he coached one of the greatest defenses in NFL history (Lawrence Taylor, Carl Banks, George Martin, Harry Carson, etc.), earning him national recognition.

Although he lettered in football, lacrosse, and squash while attending college at Wesleyan University in Middletown, Connecticut, he never played pro football.

As Pats coach, Belichick has been involved in many community events such as the March of Dimes Walk America, the Rodman Ride for Kids, RoxComp's Reading Is the Best Medicine Program and the Mayors Cup Regatta on the Charles River to benefit AccesSportAmerica, a charity dedicated to fitness of children and adults with disabilities.

CHARACTER

"In our lives we will encounter many challenges, and tomorrow we face one together. How we accept the challenge and attack the challenge head on is only about us—no one can touch that. If we win or lose this weekend, it will not make a difference in our lives. But why we play and how we play will make a difference in our lives forever."

—Beth Anders, field hockey

"The only correct actions are those that demand no explanation and no apology."

—Red Auerbach, basketball

"Show class, have pride, and display character. If you do, winning takes care of itself."

—Paul "Bear" Bryant, football

"I'd like to be remembered as—that I played the game as hard as I could. I looked for nothing. I just went out and did my job. I did it the way I knew how to do it. I didn't make any noise about it."

—Joe DiMaggio, baseball

"How you respond to the challenge in the second half will determine what you become after the game, whether you are a winner or a loser."

—Lou Holtz, football

"Always keep an open mind and a compassionate heart."

—Phil Jackson, basketball

"To be successful you have to be selfish, or else you never achieve. And once you get to your highest level, then you have to be unselfish. Stay reachable. Stay in touch. Don't isolate."

—Michael Jordan, basketball

"An Indiana player has the enthusiasm of an evangelist, the discipline of a monk, and the heart of a warrior who never loses the honesty and character of a small boy."

—Bobby Knight, basketball

"A team that has character doesn't need stimulation."

—Tom Landry, football

"Ability without character will lose. The Bills are going to be a team of high character. That stamp I will push very hard. I hope we can convey that to our fans and project something very special to the rest of the nation."

—Marv Levy, football

"It's easy to have faith in yourself and have discipline when you're a winner, when you're number one. What you've got to have is faith and discipline when you're *not yet* a winner."

—Vince Lombardi, football

"Be strong in body, clean in mind, lofty in ideals."

—James Naismith, basketball

"One of the things I love about football is that you have the full run of emotions and pressures. In fact, every chance I get to talk to any young man, I encourage him to get into athletics, football in particular. It shows you yourself. You must function under pressure. A person either faces up to what it takes or he runs away."

—Chuck Noll, football

"It's not the honor that you take with you, but the heritage you leave behind."

—Branch Rickey, baseball

VINCE LOMBARDI

Vince Lombardi was arguably the greatest coach in NFL history, but there can be no doubt that he was the best motivational speaker. He was born in Brooklyn, New York, in 1913. He played college football at Fordham. In fact, Lombardi was one of that school's legendary "Seven Blocks of Granite" in 1935 and 1936. After college he accepted his first coaching job at St. Cecilia's High School in New Jersey where he coached until 1947. He went on to be an assistant coach at Fordham, and then Army. He entered the NFL in 1954 as an assistant coach for the New York Giants. His single-wing offense helped lead Big Blue to an NFL championship in 1956. The Giants won three additional division titles during Lombardi's years there. He became the head coach and general manager of the Green Bay Packers in 1959 and led that team to NFL championships in 1961 and 1962. From 1965 to 1967, Lombardi's Packers won three consecutive NFL championships and the first two Super Bowls. Lombardi temporarily retired as a football coach after his second Super Bowl victory, and spent a year as just the GM for the Packers. He coached one year after that for the Washington Redskins before becoming ill. He died on September 3, 1970, of cancer. In ten seasons as an NFL head coach, he had a regular-season record of 105-35-6 and 9-1 in post-season play.

"Football doesn't build character. It eliminates weak ones."

—Darrell Royal, football

"You cannot attain and maintain physical condition unless you are morally and mentally conditioned. And it is impossible to be in moral condition unless you are spiritually conditioned. I always told my players that our team condition depended on two factors: how hard they worked on the floor during practice and how well they behaved between practices."

—John Wooden, basketball

CHARITY

"Any ballplayers that played for me on either the Cardinals or the Yankees could come to me if he were in need and I would give him a helping hand. I made only two exceptions—Carl Mays and Joe Bush. If they were in a gutter, I'd kick them."

—Miller Huggins, baseball

"You can't live a perfect day without doing something for someone who will never be able to repay you."

—John Wooden, basketball

CHEATING

"I believe in rules. Sure I do. If there weren't any rules, how could you break them?"

—Leo Durocher, baseball

CHEMICAL DEPENDENCY

"You can get rid of drink, but you can never get rid of smoke."

—W. G. Grace, cricket

COACHING

"This is one of the most competitive businesses there is . . . It's my life. It's my blood. It's how I'm measured."

—Bill Parcells, football

"What are coaches? Number one, we're teachers and we're educators."

—Joe Paterno, football

"Some of the greatest teaching jobs are being done by coaches that don't have very outstanding records, because they're not located in a situation where they have an opportunity to have an outstanding record. Yet they may be coming closer to getting the maximum potential out of what they have than somebody who is winning championships."

—John Wooden, basketball

COMMAND

"Some people want it to happen, some wish it would happen, others make it happen."

—Michael Jordan, basketball

"With my team I am an absolute czar. My men know it. I order plays and they obey. If they don't, I fine them."

—John McGraw, baseball

"Win or lose, I'm running this team."

—Knute Rockne, football

COMMITMENT

"Always remember, anything is yours if you are willing to pay the price. . . . One hundred percent is not enough."

—George Allen, football

"Work hard and give me your heart."

—Don Anielak, basketball

"Played wholeheartedly, football is a soul-satisfying outlet for the rugged, courageous type of boy who likes physical contact. Played halfheartedly, football is a waste of time and energy. Football is no halfway game. To play it, you have to get wet all over."

—Dana X. Bible, football

"You spend a good deal of your life gripping a baseball, and it turns out it was the other way around all the time."

—Jim Bouton, baseball

"Set a goal, adopt a plan that will help you to achieve the goal. Chances of things happening in this world without goals are slim. Make sure the goal means a lot to you. Believe that the plan is going to win. Tie to people who believe in the plan."

—Paul "Bear" Bryant, football

"I think a lot of our team commitment is a silent understanding that each one of us has poured our life into what we're doing."

—Claire Carver-Dias, synchronized swimming

"Any time you try to win everything, you must be willing to lose everything."

—Larry Csonka, football

"I come to win. If I were playing third base and my mother were rounding third with the run that was going to beat us, I'd trip her. Oh, I'd pick her up and brush her off and say, 'Sorry, Mom,' but nobody beats me."

—Leo Durocher, baseball

"A total commitment is paramount to reaching the ultimate in performance."

—Tom Flores, football

"Those who truly have the spirit of champions are never wholly happy with an easy win. Half the satisfaction stems from knowing that it was the time and the effort you invested that led to your high achievement."

—Nicole Haislett, swimming

"Many people flounder about in life because they do not have a purpose, an objective toward which to work. . . . You can achieve only that which you will do."

—George Halas, football

"It's tough enough getting that boat ashore with everybody rowing, let alone when a guy stands up and starts putting his jacket on."

—Lou Holtz, football

"I believe in playing with your heart, with every fiber in your body—fairly, squarely, by the rules—to win. And I believe that any man's finest moment, the greatest fulfillment of all he holds dear, is that moment when he has worked his heart out and lies exhausted on the floor of battle—victorious."

—Bela Karolyi, gymnastics

"Believe that the loose ball that you are chasing has your name on it."

—Mike Krzyzewski, basketball

"The quality of a person's life is in direct proportion to their commitment to excellence, regardless of their chosen field of endeavor."

—Vince Lombardi, football

"The road to Easy Street goes through the sewer."

—John Madden, football

"Good things happen to those who hustle."

—Chuck Noll, football

"I want to be remembered as the guy who gave his all whenever he was on the field."

—Hakeem Olajuwon, basketball

"For committing yourself to winning the game, whether you win it or not, you always play in blood and tears."

—Joe Paterno, football

"There are only two options regarding commitment. You're either *in* or you're *out*. There's no such thing as life in-between."

—Pat Riley, basketball

"Commitment is like ham and eggs. The chicken makes a contribution. The pig makes a commitment."

—Fred Shero, hockey

"Let's put it this way: if one of my brothers were standing in front of the bus last night and we were about to leave and he was on the other team, I'd have run over him. I wouldn't have called out first to ask him to get out of the way, either. That's my mentality, that's the way it is. I don't really care."

—Brian Sutter, hockey

"No matter what business you're in, you can't run in place or someone will pass you by. It doesn't matter how many games you've won."

—Jim Valvano, basketball

"The bigger the price you pay for something, the harder it is to give up on it."

—Bob Williams, basketball

"What you lack in talent can be made up with desire, hustle, and giving 110 percent all the time."

—Don Zimmer, baseball

COMMUNICATION

"Young people want you to be real with them."

—Earvin "Magic" Johnson, basketball

"Effective teamwork begins and ends with communication. Communication does not always occur naturally, even among a tight-knit group of individuals. Communication must be taught and practiced in order to bring everyone together as one."

—Mike Krzyzewski, basketball

COMPASSION

"The answer is surprisingly simple. Just do right. Live an honorable life. Do your best. Treat others as you want to be treated."

—Lou Holtz, football

"Once you've done the mental work, there comes a point you have to throw yourself into the action and put your heart on the line. That means not only being brave, but being compassionate towards yourself, your teammates, and your opponents."

—Phil Jackson, basketball

COMPENSATION

"People who create 20 percent of the results will begin believing they deserve 80 percent of the rewards."

—Pat Riley, basketball

COMPETITION

"If you're a competitive person, that stays with you. You don't stop. You always look over your shoulder."

—Earvin "Magic" Johnson, basketball

"I play to win, whether during practice or a real game. And I will not let anything get in the way of me and my competitive enthusiasm to win."

—Michael Jordan, basketball

"You don't play against opponents, you play against the game of basketball."

—Bobby Knight, basketball

"What counts in sports is not the victory, but the magnificence of the struggle."

—Joe Paterno, football

"I don't care how good you play, you can find somebody who can beat you, and I don't care how bad you play, you can find somebody you can beat."

—Harvey Penick, golf

"I think there should be bad blood between all clubs."

—Earl Weaver, baseball

COMPLACENCY

"If what you have done yesterday still looks big to you, you haven't done much today."

—Mike Krzyzewski, basketball

"The odds are always against you no matter what your previous history is. You have to overcome the tendency to relax."

—Tom Osborne, football

"When a great team loses through complacency, it will constantly search for new and more intricate explanations to explain away defeat."

—Pat Riley, basketball

CONCENTRATION

"Basketball is like photography: if you don't focus, all you have is the negative."

—Dan Frisby, basketball

"Competitive sports are played mainly on a five-and-a-half-inch court, the space between your ears."

—Bobby Jones, golf

"Everybody hears, but few listen."

—Bobby Knight, basketball

"Concentration is the ability to think about absolutely nothing when it is absolutely necessary."

—Ray Knight, baseball

"I don't believe you can be emotional and concentrate the way you should to be effective. As a team, we win by concentrating, by thinking. The players don't want to see me running around and screaming. They want to believe that I know what I am doing."

—Tom Landry, football

"When you are out there on the soccer field playing, nothing else matters at the time. It's like the whole world has disappeared, and you and your teammates are all that matters."

—Amber Massey, soccer

"There can only be one state of mind as you approach any profound test: total concentration, a spirit of togetherness, and strength."

—Pat Riley, basketball

"We can all be geniuses because one definition of genius is the infinite capacity for taking pains. Perfection in petty detail is most essential. Generalities don't count and won't help you in football."

—Knute Rockne, football

"When you're riding, only the race in which you're riding is important."

—Willie Shoemaker, jockey

"There are one hundred and ninety-nine ways to get beat, but only one way to win; get there first."

—Willie Shoemaker, jockey

"Hitting is 50 percent above the shoulders."

—Ted Williams, baseball

"When I go out on the ice, I just think about my skating. I forget it is a competition."

—Katarina Witt, figure skating

CONFIDENCE

"Trust in yourself. That belief that you can do it. Trust in yourself you believe that you can respond in any circumstance. . . . You see it's that trust, that last little *oomph* in the delivery that makes all the difference. It all comes back to trusting in yourself and the work you have done. You are ready for this—bring it on. There are times when you're tired and times when you don't believe in yourself. That's when you have to stick it out and draw on the confidence that you have deep down beneath all the doubts and worries"

—Jim Abbott, baseball (Abbott is the only major league baseball player to be born with one hand)

"Just do what you do best."

—Red Auerbach, basketball

"These players, a lot of other people didn't believe in them, but they believe in themselves. And that is all that matters."

—Bill Belichick, football

"I never blame myself when I'm not hitting. I just blame the bat and if it keeps up I change bats. After all, if I know it isn't my fault that I'm not hitting, how can I get mad at myself."

—Yogi Berra, baseball

"What's the worst thing that can happen to a quarterback? He loses his confidence."

—Terry Bradshaw, football

"What are you doing here? Tell me why you are here. If you are not here to win a national championship, you're in the wrong place. You boys are special. I don't want you players to be like other students. I want special people. You can learn a lot on the football field that isn't taught in the home, the church, or the classroom. There are going to be days when you think you've got no more to give and then you're going to give plenty more. You are going to have pride and class. You are going to be very special. You are going to win the national championship for Alabama."

—Paul "Bear" Bryant, football

"I remember when I was in college, people told me I couldn't play in the NBA. There's always somebody saying you can't do it, and those people have to be ignored."

—Bill Cartwright, basketball

BILL CARTWRIGHT

Bill Cartwright was a star college player for the University of San Francisco Dons, where he was a three-time All-American and three-time West Coast Conference Player of the Year. He was named one of the West Coast Conference's Fifty Greatest Student Athletes of All Time. He was drafted third overall in the 1979 NBA draft. He was the New York Knicks first-round pick that year, and he ended up being the Knicks center from 1979–1988. In 1980 he was named to the NBA's All-Rookie team and was named to the 1980 NBA Eastern Conference All-Star team. Called Mr. Bill because of the popular *Saturday Night Live* character at the time, Cartwright had his best year statistically that rookie season when he averaged 21.7 points and 8.9 rebounds per game. But he developed into a quiet leader on the team during the rest of his time in New York. On June 27, 1988, Chicago obtained Cartwright from the Knicks in exchange for Charles Oakley. In Chicago, Bill won enough championship rings for four fingers and a thumb. Cartwright helped the Bulls to at least 55 victories in each of his final five seasons in Chicago—of course, the fact that Michael Jordan was on the team had something to do with that as well. Cartwright played six seasons in all for the Bulls, and finished up with one season in Seattle, 1994–1995. Cartwright returned to school in the 1990s at his *alma mater*. In 1994, he earned his Master's Degree in Organizational Development and Human Resources from San Francisco. He was hired on September 3, 1996, to be the assistant coach for the Chicago Bulls and spent six seasons in that position before becoming the Bulls' head coach for two years. As an assistant coach he was in charge of the Bulls' big men. His protégé Elton Brand won the NBA Rookie of the Year Award in 2000. Mr. Bill joined the New Jersey Nets staff as an assistant coach on August 27, 2004. In 2006 his primary job on the Nets was to be the personal coach to Serbian center Nenad Krstic. About his coach Nenad said, "He has helped me a lot. He always talks to me—especially on post moves. If I made some mistake he will tell me all the time, 'You should do this. You should do that.'" Nets head coach Lawrence Frank credits Cartwright with the improvement in Krstic's play: "So many things you see Nenad do on the court, it's an unbelievable amount of repetition that he's done with Bill." Bill and his wife Sheri have four children—Justin, Jason, James, and Kristin.

"Before you can win, you have to believe you are worthy."

—Mike Ditka, football

"I guess I was never much in awe of anybody. I think you have to have that attitude if you're going to go far in this game."

—Bob Gibson, baseball

"Belief in oneself is one of the most important bricks in building any successful venture."

—Frank Gifford, football

"When you win the boss—bat. If you are in doubt, think about it—then bat. If you have very big doubts, consult a colleague—then bat."

—W. G. Grace, legendary nineteenth-century cricketeer

"One-hundred percent of shots not taken don't go in."

—Wayne Gretzky, hockey

"I don't like to sound egotistical, but every time I stepped up to the plate with a bat in my hands, I couldn't help but feel sorry for the pitcher."

—Rogers Hornsby, baseball

"Positive thinking is the key to success in business, education, pro football, anything that you can mention. I go out there thinking that I'm going to complete every pass."

—Ron Jaworski, football

"I'm the best defensive end around. I'd hate to have to play against me."

—Deacon Jones, football

"I've never been afraid to fail. I never looked at the consequences of missing a big shot . . . when you think about the consequences you always think of a negative result."

—Michael Jordan, basketball

"Part of being a champ is acting like a champ. You have to learn how to win and not run away when you lose. Everyone has bad stretches and real successes. Either way, you have to be careful not to lose your confidence or get too confident."

—Nancy Kerrigan, figure skating

"Confidence shared is better than confidence only in yourself."

—Mike Krzyzewski, basketball

"Confidence builds slowly, but once you get there, confidence breeds confidence."

—Marv Levy, football

"Confidence is contagious and so is lack of confidence, and a customer will recognize both."

—Vince Lombardi, football

MIKE KRZYZEWSKI

Mike Krzyzewski (pronounced Sha-shef-ski) was born in Chicago on February 13, 1947, the son of an elevator operator and a cleaning woman. Mike was a star basketball player in high school and went to the U.S. Military Academy where he played under head coach Bobby Knight. During his five years in the army, he was head coach of the U.S. Military Academy Prep School in Belvoir, Virginia. He resigned from the army in 1974 and became an assistant coach at Indiana under his old coach Bobby Knight. He left that job to become Army's head coach and, in 1980, became head coach at Duke, the job he has had ever since. In 1984 he led Duke to its first NCAA tournament. The Blue Devils have made it to "the dance" just about every year since. From 1988 to 1992, his teams went to the Final Four for five consecutive seasons, and in 1991 Duke won its first national championship. In 1992, the team went wire-to-wire at the number-one position in the rankings and won its second consecutive national championship. In 1992 he was named Sportsman of the Year by *The Sporting News*, the only coach ever to receive that honor. The Blue Devils lost in the finals of the NCAA tournament in 1994, losing to Arkansas. Under Coach K, Duke has made it to the Final Four nine times. In 2001, Duke won their third national championship. Today, Mike Krzyzewski lives in Durham, North Carolina, where he and his wife Mickie have been active in community campaigns against drug abuse and drunk driving. The coach and Mrs. Krzyzewski are co-chairs of the Duke Children's Miracle Network Telethon.

"I think it's the mark of a great player to be confident in tough situations."

—John McEnroe, tennis

"I've got news for you. We're gonna win the game. I guarantee it."

—Joe Namath, football

"If you have confidence you have patience. Confidence, that is everything."

—Ilie Nastase, tennis

"Losing a game is heartbreaking. Losing your sense of excellence or worth is a tragedy."

—Joe Paterno, football

"My mother taught me very early to believe I could achieve any accomplishment I wanted to. The first was to walk without braces."

—Wilma Rudolph, track and field

"To be successful, you don't have to do extraordinary things. Just do ordinary things extraordinarily well."

—John Rohn, basketball

"Never let the fear of striking out get in your way."

—Babe Ruth, baseball

"What the mind can conceive, the mind can achieve, and those who stay will be champions."

—Bo Schembechler, football

"Experience tells you what to do; confidence allows you to do it."

—Stanley Roger "Stan" Smith, tennis

"I've always believed no matter how many shots I miss, I'm going to make the next one."

—Isiah Thomas, basketball

"I always felt that I was as good as the next person, and I didn't care what they had."

—Lenny Wilkens, basketball

ISIAH THOMAS

One of the greatest guards ever, Isiah spent his entire playing career with the Detroit Pistons, playing from 1981–1994. He played on two NBA championship teams and was once named the MVP of the finals. He led the league once in scoring and twice in assists. Twice he was named the MVP of the NBA All-Star Game. Isiah, who was inducted into the Basketball Hall of Fame in 2000, was an NBA head coach for three seasons, leading the Indiana Pacers to a 131-115 regular season and 6-10 postseason record from 2000–2003. He became the Knicks president of basketball operations on December 22, 2003. His busy duties expanded on June 22, 2006, when he replaced Larry Brown as head coach. He currently lives in Purchase, New York, where the Knicks also hold their pre-season training camp. He married his college sweetheart, the former Lynn Kendall, in 1985. The Thomases have a son and a daughter: Josh and Lauren.

"The Babe is here. Who wants to come in second?"

—Mildred "Babe" Didrikson Zaharias, golf

CONFRONTATION

"Confrontation simply means meeting the truth head-on."

—Mike Krzyzewski, basketball

CONTROL

"Just take the ball and throw it where you want to. Throw strikes. Home plate don't move."

—Leroy "Satchel" Paige, baseball

COURAGE

"He doesn't know the meaning of the word fear, but then again he doesn't know the meaning of most words."

—Bobby Bowden, football

"There's no substitute for guts."

—Paul "Bear" Bryant, football

"Courage and confidence are what decision making is all about. It takes courage not only to make decisions, but to live with those decisions afterward."

—Mike Krzyzewski, basketball

"Get in front of those balls, you won't get hurt. That's what you've got a chest for, young man."

—John McGraw, baseball

"Success is never final. Failure is never fatal. It's courage that counts."

—John Wooden, basketball

CRISES

"In a crisis, don't hide behind anything or anybody. They are going to find you anyway."

—Paul "Bear" Bryant, football

"I believe God gave us crises for some reason—and it certainly wasn't for us to say that everything about them is bad. A crisis can be a momentous time for a team to grow—if a leader handles it properly."

—Mike Krzyzewski, basketball

CRITICISM, RESPONSE TO

"People react to criticism in different ways, and my way is definitely to come out fighting."

—David Beckham, soccer

CURIOSITY

"I never learn anything talking. I only learn things when I ask questions."

—Lou Holtz, football

DANCING

"Football isn't a contact sport, it's a collision sport. Dancing is a contact sport."

—Duffy Daugherty, football

DEATH

"There's a little prayer I always say whenever I think of my family, or when I'm flying, when I'm afraid, and I am afraid of flying. It's just a little one. You can say it no matter what, whether you're Catholic or Jewish or Protestant or whatever. And I've probably said it a thousand times since I heard the news about Thurman Munson. I'm not trying to be maudlin or anything . . . but this is just a little one I say time and time again. It's just: 'Angel of God, Thurman's guardian dear, to whom his love commits him here, there, or everywhere, ever this night and day be at his side, to light and guard, to rule and guide.' For some reason it makes me feel like I'm talking to Thurman, or whoever's name you put in there, whether it be my wife or any of my children, my parents or anything. It's just something to keep you from going bananas, because if you keep thinking about what happened, and you can't understand it, that's what really drives you to despair. Faith. You got to have faith. They say that time heals all wounds, and I don't quite agree with that one hundred percent. Time gets you to cope with wounds. You carry them the rest of your life."

—Phil Rizzuto, baseball

DEDICATION

"Many, many times, the kids with the less talent become the better athletes because they're more dedicated to achieving their full potential."

—Red Auerbach, basketball

"One thing will never change—we will be going out to win."

—David Beckham, soccer

"If you believe in yourself and have dedication and pride—and never quit—you'll be a winner. The price of victory is high, but so are the rewards."

—Paul "Bear" Bryant, football

"I bleed Dodger blue and when I die, I'm going to the big Dodger in the sky."

—Tommy Lasorda, baseball

"In order to excel, you must be completely dedicated to your chosen sport. You must also be prepared to work hard and be willing to accept constructive criticism. Without a total 100 percent dedication, you won't be able to do this."

—Willie Mays, baseball

"The winning team has a dedication. It will have a core of veteran players who set the standards. They will not accept defeat."

—Merlin Olsen, football

DEFENSE

"In all the researching you do as a coach, studying other coaches and championship-type situations, you find that all those teams combined talent with great defense. You've got to stop other teams to win."

—Pat Riley, basketball

"You never lose a game if the opponent doesn't score."

—Darrell Royal, football

DELIVERING BAD NEWS

"You got a hundred more young kids than you have a place for on the club. Every one of them has had a going-away party. They have been given the shaving kit and the $50. They kissed everybody and said, 'See you in the majors in two years.' You see these poor kids who shouldn't be here in the first place. You write on the report card, '4-4-4 and out.' That's the lowest rating in everything. Then you call them and say, 'It's a consensus among us that we're going to let you go back home.' Some of them cry, some get mad, but none of them will leave until you answer them one question, 'Skipper, what do you think?' And you got to look every one of those kids in the eye and kick their dreams in the ass and say no. If you say it mean enough, maybe they do themselves a favor and don't waste years learning what you can see in a day. They don't have what it takes to make the majors, just like I never had it."

—Earl Weaver, baseball

DESIRE

"You're still going to win with preparation and dedication and plain old desire. If you don't have enough genuine desire, you won't be dedicated enough to prepare properly."

—Paul "Bear" Bryant, football

"Give me some scratching, diving, hungry ballplayers who come to kill you."

—Leo Durocher, baseball

"If you're a champion, you have to have it in your heart."

—Chris Evert, tennis

"I'd catch a punt naked, in the snow, in Buffalo, for a chance to play in the NFL."

—Steve Henderson, football

"I've always played hard. If that's rough and tough, I can't help it. I don't believe there's any such thing as a good loser. I wouldn't sit down and play a game of cards with you right now without wanting to win. If I hadn't felt that way I wouldn't have got very far in baseball."

—Rogers Hornsby, baseball

"Parity is not the American Way. The American Way is to dominate somebody else."

—Davey Johnson, baseball

"Failure, to me, is not having the desire to try. Having the desire to try is in its own way success."

—Bobby Knight, basketball

"Winning isn't everything—but wanting to win is."

—Vince Lombardi, football

"In playing or managing, the game of ball is only fun for me when I'm out in front and winning. I don't give a hill of beans for the rest of the game."

—John McGraw, baseball

"A boy shows how much he wants to play in the spring, when it's tough, and during two-a-days, when it's hot and tough."

—Darrell Royal, football

DETAILS

"There's nothing wrong with setting goals, but it doesn't mean a thing if you don't pay attention to the day-to-day details."

—Don Shula, football

DETERMINATION

"People of mediocre ability sometimes achieve outstanding success because they don't know when to quit. Most men succeed because they are determined to."

—George Allen, football

"The one that makes you proud is the one who isn't good enough to play, but it means so much to him, he puts so much into it, that he plays anyway. I have had a lot of those, and I can coach them better than most."

—Paul "Bear" Bryant, football

"The vision of a champion is someone who is bent over, drenched in sweat, at the point of exhaustion when no one else is watching."

—Anson Dorrance, soccer

"Don't be a spectator, don't let life pass you by."

—Lou Holtz, football

"I'd run over my own mother to win the Super Bowl."

—Joe Jacoby, football

"The difference between the impossible and the possible lies in a man's determination."

—Tommy Lasorda, baseball

"If you're not going to play to win, you might as well hold the Olympics in someone's back yard."

—Jesse Owens, track and field

DISCIPLINE

"Discipline is 90 percent anticipation."

—Woody Hayes, football

"Discipline and concentration are a matter of being interested."

—Tom Kite, golf

"Discipline is doing what you are supposed to do in the best possible manner at the time you are supposed to do it."

—Mike Krzyzewski, basketball

"Most successful players not only accept rules and limitations, I believe they need them. In fact, I believe players are free to perform at their best only when they know what the expectations are and where the limits stand."

—Tom Landry, football

"The good Lord gave you a body that can stand most anything. It's your mind you have to convince."

—Vince Lombardi, football

"A team should never practice on a field that is not lined. Your players have to become aware of the field's boundaries."

—John Madden, football

"As coaches, we represent one of the few remaining organized systems for demanding discipline of young men. Their education will not be complete if it does not include the discipline and generosity that can come from being a team member, if it does not include an awareness of responsibility to others. We are 'people coaches,' not just 'football coaches.'"

—Ara Parseghian, football

"Discipline is not a nasty word."

—Pat Riley, basketball

"Pitchers did me a favor when they knocked me down. It made me more determined. I wouldn't let that pitcher get me out. They say you can't hit if you are on your back but I didn't hit on my back—I got up."

—Frank Robinson, baseball

"To teach anything, you must have order. To have order, you must have discipline. That means rules that are enforced. But we have torn down any form of accountability for our children. These days you almost have to go to court to get in a child's face. And some of these kids need somebody in their face. Adults feel they have to apologize for being authority figures. People say the teachers are not dedicated. That is not true. They are afraid. Their hands are tied. They feel like they need an attorney."

—John Thompson, basketball

DISCRIMINATION

"Racial bigotry is nothing but pure ignorance, not to mention hate, and if my vocabulary was bigger, I could probably come up with some better words to describe it."

—Bobby Bowden, football

"There is no room in baseball for discrimination. It is our national pastime and a game for all."

—Lou Gehrig, baseball

DIVINE INTERVENTION

"If God let you hit a home run last time up, then who struck you out the time before that?"

—Sparky Anderson, baseball

"A fellow has to have faith in God above and Rollie Fingers in the bullpen."

—Alvin Dark, baseball

"I'd like to thank the Lord for making me a Yankee."

—Joe DiMaggio, baseball

"God watches over drunks and third basemen."

—Leo Durocher, baseball

"As we look down through history, we find out that God, at certain points, picks very average men and women, and what he does is give them a life, gives them some talent, surrounds them with great people, and guides them to some achievement."

—Joe Gibbs, football

"God doesn't interfere."

—Tom Landry, football

"We don't pray to win. We pray to play the best we can, and to keep us free from injury. And the prayer we say after the game is one of thanksgiving."

—Vince Lombardi, football

"You do a lot of praying, but most of the time the answer is no."

—John McKay, football

"When it comes to football, God is prejudiced—toward big, fast kids."

—Chuck Mills, football

"I've found that prayers work best when you have big players."

—Knute Rockne, football

"I had hoped God would be neutral."

—Darrell Royal, football

DOING WHAT'S BEST FOR THE TEAM

"Perhaps the toughest call for a coach is weighing what is best for an individual against what is best for the team. Keeping a player on the roster just because I liked him personally, or even because of his great contributions to the team in the past, when I felt someone else could do more for the team, would be a disservice to the team's goals."

—Tom Landry, football

DOUBLEHEADERS

"I love doubleheaders. That way I get to keep my uniform on longer."

—Tommy Lasorda, baseball

DREAMS

"We grew up as kids having dreams. But now we're too sophisticated as adults, as a nation. We stopped dreaming. We should always have dreams."

—Herb Brooks, hockey

"You think the greatest thing in the whole world would be to become a baseball player. If the best thing has already happened, what's next?"

—John McGraw, baseball

"Reach high, for stars lie hidden in your soul. Dream deep, for every dream precedes the goal."

—Ralph Vaull Starr, author

"If you shoot for the stars and hit the moon, it's OK. But you've got to shoot for something. A lot of people don't even shoot."

—Robert Townsend, filmmaker

"Be a dreamer. If you don't know how to dream, you're dead."

—Jim Valvano, basketball

"We should never discourage young people from dreaming dreams."

—Lenny Wilkens, basketball

EDUCATION

"It's what you learn after you know it all that counts."

—John Wooden, basketball

EFFICIENCY

"A particular shot or way of moving the ball can be a player's personal signature, but efficiency of performance is what wins the game for the team."

—Pat Riley, basketball

EFFORT

You find that you have peace of mind and can enjoy yourself, get more sleep, rest when you know that it was a 100 percent effort that you gave—win or lose."

—Gordie Howe, hockey

"I can accept failure, but I can't accept not trying. I've always believed that if you put in the work, the results will come. I don't do things half-heartedly. Because I know if I do, then I can expect half-hearted results."

—Michael Jordan, basketball

"There are three types of baseball players: those who make it happen, those who watch it happen, and those who wonder what happens."

—Tommy Lasorda, baseball

"Leaders are made, they are not born. They are made by hard effort, which is the price which all of us must pay to achieve any goal that is worthwhile."

—Vince Lombardi, football

"The team that gets off to a good start wins pennants."

—John McGraw, baseball

"If you want to win a race you have to go a little berserk."

—Bill Rodgers, track and field

"There are not traffic jams along the extra mile."

—Roger Staubach, football

"All I ask is that you bust your hiney on that field."

—Casey Stengel, baseball

"If you want it, you've got to give it."

—Lenny Wilkens, basketball

"Don't measure yourself by what you have accomplished, but what you should have accomplished with your ability."

—John Wooden, basketball

EGO

"The only players I hurt with my words are the ones who have an inflated opinion of their ability."

—Bill Parcells, football

ELEMENT OF SURPRISE

"If a team cannot perform with excellence at a moment's notice, they probably will fail in the long run."

—Mike Krzyzewski, basketball

ENDURANCE

"The man who can drive himself further once the effort gets painful is the man who will win."

—Roger Bannister, track and field

"There never was a man on Earth who pitched as much as me. But the more I pitched, the stronger my arm would get."

—Leroy "Satchel" Paige, baseball

"I'm an early guy and a late guy."

—Ray Rhodes, football

"In our day, when a pitcher got into trouble in a game, instead of taking him out, our manager would leave him in and tell him to pitch his way out of it."

—Cy Young, baseball

EXCELLENCE

"Perfection is not attainable. But if we chase perfection, we can catch excellence."

—Vince Lombardi, football

"Excellence is the unlimited ability to improve the quality of what you have to offer."

—Rick Pitino, basketball

"Excellence is the gradual result of always striving to do better."

—Pat Riley, basketball

EXCUSES

"The trouble with athletes today is that they are great at rationalizing. Too many won't stand up and take the blame. When one does, you have a rare man."

—Hubie Brown, basketball

"There's no such thing as coulda, shoulda, or woulda. If you shoulda and coulda, you woulda done it."

—Pat Riley, basketball

RICK PITINO

Pitino has been a successful basketball coach at both the college and pro levels. Rick began his coaching career as an assistant at the University of Hawaii from 1974–1976. In 1976 he became an assistant coach at Syracuse University, cutting his honeymoon short in order to take the job and carry out his first assignment—the successful recruiting of Louis Orr. Since then he has also coached Boston University, Providence College, and the University of Kentucky (1989–1997). Since 2001 he's been the head coach at the University of Louisville. He has coached more than forty NCAA tournament games and has won more than three-quarters of them. Pitino's first NBA coaching gig was as Knicks head coach from July 13, 1987, until 1989. As head coach of the Knicks he was preceded by Bob Hill and brought a whole new style to the team. Up until that time, the Knicks had played a half-court game—a lot of designed plays, but a team that walked the ball up the court. There would be none of that under the Pitino regime. He taught a style of basketball that involved running, running, running—and a healthy shower of threes. In the NBA, he also coached the Celtics from 1997–2001.

As a schoolboy Rick was captain of the St. Dominic's High School basketball team in Oyster Bay, Long Island. He was also a standout guard at the University of Massachusetts, where he was also captain of the team. He graduated from the University of Massachusetts in 1974. He has since been inducted into the the University of Massachusetts Hall of Fame and his 329 career assists there still rank sixth-best on the school's all-time list.

EXECUTION

"An acre of performance is worth a whole world of promise."

—Red Auerbach, basketball

"You can play hard. You can play aggressive. You can give 120 percent, but if one guy is out of position then someone's running through the line of scrimmage and he's going to gain a bunch of yards."

—Bill Belichick, football

EXPECTATIONS

"If you accept the expectations of others, especially negative ones, then you never will change the outcome. . . . You have to expect things of yourself before you can do them."

—Michael Jordan, basketball

"The more successful you become, the longer the yardstick people use to measure you by."

—Tom Landry, football

EXPERIENCE

"I'm just a simple plowhand from Arkansas, but I have learned over the years how to hold a team together—how to lift some men up, how to calm others down, until finally they've got one heartbeat, together, a team."

—Paul "Bear" Bryant, football

"I don't think you win because you have more experience or that you've been there before. You go out and play the game."

—Marv Levy, football

EXPLANATIONS

"I learned this about coaching: You don't have to explain victory and you can't explain defeat."

—Darrell Royal, football

FAILURE

"I've missed more than 9,000 shots in my career. I've lost almost 300 games. Twenty-six times, I've been trusted to take the game winning shot and missed. I've failed over and over and over again in my life. And that is why I succeed."

—Michael Jordan, basketball

"Success is never final, but failure can be."

—Bill Parcells, football

"Giving yourself permission to lose guarantees a loss."

—Pat Riley, basketball

"Baseball is the only field of endeavor where a man can succeed three times out of ten and be considered a good performer."

—Ted Williams, baseball

FAIR PLAY

"Don't play dumb and don't play dirty."

—Marv Levy, football

FAITH

"When I was younger, I thought that the key to success was just hard work. But the real foundation is faith. Faith—the idea that 'I can do it'—is the opposite of fear ('What if I fail?'). And faith creates motivation which in turn leads to commitment, hard work, preparation . . . and eventually success."

—Howard Twilley, football

FAITHFULNESS

"I plan on staying at Alabama for the rest of my career. I guarantee that I'll be here for you through it all, regardless of what happens."

—Paul "Bear" Bryant, football

"Dance with the one that brung ya."

—Darrell Royal, football

FANS

"I always thought there was at least one person in the stands who had never seen me play, and I didn't want to let him down."

—Joe DiMaggio, baseball

"It was Brooklyn against the world. They were not only complete fanatics, but they knew baseball like the fans of no other city. It was exciting to play there. It was a treat. I walked into that crummy, flyblown park as Brooklyn manager for nine years, and every time I entered my pulse quickened and my spirits soared."

—Leo Durocher, baseball

"Any player that don't sign autographs for little kids ain't an American. He's a communist."

—Rogers Hornsby, baseball

"Always give an autograph when somebody asks you."

—Tommy Lasorda, baseball

FEAR

"Show me a guy who's afraid to look bad, and I'll show you a guy you can beat every time."

—Lou Brock, baseball

"Football has never been just a game to me. Never. I knew it from the time it got me out of Moro Bottom, Arkansas—and that's one of the things that motivated me, the fear of going back to plowing and driving those mules and chopping cotton for fifty cents a day."

—Paul "Bear" Bryant, football

"I know fear is an obstacle for some people, but it is an illusion to me. Failure always made me try harder next time."

—Michael Jordan, basketball

"Why did I want to win? Because I didn't want to lose!"

—Max Schmelling, boxing

FLEXIBILITY

"Once you are labeled 'the best' you want to stay up there, and you can't do it by loafing around. If I don't keep changing. I'm history."

—Larry Bird, basketball

"If you are going to win games, you had better be ready to adapt."

—Scotty Bowman, hockey

"Failure is not fatal, but failure to change might be."

—John Wooden, basketball

FOCUS

"Try not to do too many things at once. Know what you want, the number-one thing today and tomorrow. Persevere and get it done."

—George Allen, football

"Winning is important to me, but what brings me real joy is the experience of being fully engaged in whatever I'm doing."

—Phil Jackson, basketball

"Success demands singleness of purpose. Success is like anything worthwhile. It has a price."

—Vince Lombardi, football

FRATERNIZATION

"You don't kiss your enemy. You see, theoretically, if I'm playing against you, if you make me look bad and I get fired, you're my enemy. That means you're taking the food out of my mouth, out of my family's mouth. So as long as you're my enemy, let's be enemies."

—Red Auerbach, basketball

"Buy a steak for a player on another club after the game, but don't even speak to him on the field. Get out there and beat them to death."

—Leo Durocher, baseball

"There's no way you can go barreling into second and dump a guy on a double play—like you should do—when you've been fraternizing with him before a game."

—Frank Robinson, baseball

FRIENDSHIP

"When you need a friend, you can always count on your teammates."

—Jim Brown, football

"Friendships are forgotten when the game begins."

—Alvin Dark, baseball

"When you face a crisis, you know who your true friends are."

—Earvin "Magic" Johnson, basketball

"You have to work hard at staying in contact with your friends so that the relationships will continue and live on . . . Friendships, along with love, make life worth living."

—Mike Krzyzewski, basketball

FUN

"Remember that sports are meant to be fun. Don't let someone make the sport unfun for you."

—A.J. Kitt, downhill skiing

"Just play. Have fun. Enjoy the game."

—Michael Jordan, basketball

"Winning is only half of it. Having fun winning is the other half."

—Bum Phillips, football

"I'm at the stage of my career when it's not only about winning and developing players, it's about having fun."

—Rick Pitino, basketball

FUNDAMENTALS

"Build your empire on the firm foundation of the fundamentals."

—Lou Holtz, football

THE FUTURE

"Today, you have 100 percent of your life left."

—Tom Landry, football

"The only points you can be dead sure of are those you've already made."

—Byron Nelson, golf

GENEROSITY

"Basketball is sharing."

—Phil Jackson, basketball

GENIUS

"Nobody in football should be called a genius. A genius is a guy like Norman Einstein."

—Joe Theismann, football

THE GIPPER

"Well, boys. . . . I haven't a thing to say. Played a great game . . . all of you. Great game. I guess we just can't expect to win them all. I'm going to tell you something I've kept to myself for years. . . . None of you ever knew George Gipp. It was long before your time. But you know what a tradition he is at Notre Dame. . . . And the last thing he said to me, 'Rock,' he said, 'sometime, when the team is up against it—and the breaks are beating the boys—tell them to go out there with all they got and win just one for the Gipper. . . . I don't know where I'll be then, Rock', he said, 'but I'll know about it—and I'll be happy.' Well. What are we waiting for?"

—Knute Rockne, football

"Uh, you, uh, all know that we hand out a game ball to the outstanding player. Well, I'd like to change that. We just got word that Brian Piccolo is—that's he's sick, very sick. And, it

KNUTE ROCKNE (1888–1931)

Originally from Norway, Knute Rockne and his family came to America when he was five. He attended Notre Dame University beginning in 1910, and despite being only 5'8", 145 lbs., he was the starting end on the football team and was named third-team All-American his senior year. That year the Fighting Irish defeated Army 35-13, largely because of the passes Rockne caught downfield. After graduation he stayed on at Notre Dame as assistant football coach and chemistry teacher. He became the Irish head football coach in 1918. Perhaps his greatest years were 1921–1924 when his team featured the Four Horsemen in their offensive backfield. The 1924 team went undefeated and bested Stanford in the Rose Bowl. In 1928 the Irish were trailing Army 6-0 at the half-time when Rockne motivated his players to victory by telling them of George Gipp, a player who had died of pneumonia. The team did indeed win one for the Gipper. Rockne's final two Irish teams in 1929 and 1930 went undefeated. He died on March 31, 1931, when a plane he was a passenger on from Kansas City to Los Angeles crashed in Kansas. When his casket was trained back to Illinois, an estimated 10,000 people showed up at the Chicago train station to see it. His legacy included the success of his former players, twenty-three of whom went on to become head coaches themselves.

looks like he might never play football again, or for a long time. And, I think we should dedicate ourselves to give our maximum effort to win this game and give the game ball to 'Pic.' We can all sign it. And take it up. . . . "

—Gayle Sayers, football

GIVING YOUR BEST

"If you put your effort and concentration into playing to your potential, to be the best that you can be, I don't care what the scoreboard says at the end of the game, in my book we're gonna be winners."

—Coach Norman Dale, basketball (from the movie *Hoosiers*, 1986. Angelo Pizzo, scriptwriter)

"Nobody who ever gave his best regretted it."

—George Halas, football

"I won't accept anything less than the best a player's capable of doing . . . and he has the right to expect the best that I can do for him and the team!"

—Lou Holtz, football

"I've always made a total effort, even when the odds seemed entirely against me. I never quit trying; I never felt that I didn't have a chance to win."

—Arnold Palmer, golf

"Victory isn't defined by wins or losses. It is defined by effort. If you can truthfully say, 'I did the best I could, I gave everything I had,' then you're a winner."

—Wolfgang Schadler, luge

"Success comes from knowing that you did your best to become the best that you are capable of becoming."

—John Wooden, basketball

GOALS

"Find something you love, and go after it, with all of your heart."

—Jim Abbott, baseball

"If you don't know where you are going, you will wind up somewhere else."

—Yogi Berra, baseball

"Goals determine what you're going to be."

—Julius Erving, basketball

"If you're bored with life—you don't get up every morning with a burning desire to do things—you don't have enough goals."

—Lou Holtz, football

"To achieve in sports you first have to have a dream, and then you must act on that dream. The best athletes are those who truly enjoy what they are doing and display a tremendous amount of work ethic. They continue to persevere in spite of setbacks and never lose sight of their ultimate goal."

—Dianne Holum, speed skating

"Set your goals high, and don't stop till you get there."

—Bo Jackson, football and baseball

"You're the only one who can make the difference. Whatever your dream is, go for it."

—Earvin "Magic" Johnson, basketball

"Goals should be realistic, attainable, and shared among all members of the team."

—Mike Krzyzewski, basketball

"Setting a goal is not the main thing. It is deciding how you will go about achieving it and staying with that plan."

—Tom Landry, football

"Don't let other people tell you what you want."

—Pat Riley, basketball

"The most important thing about motivation is goal setting. You should always have a goal."

—Francie Larrieu Smith, cross country

"How do you go from where you are to where you want to be? And I think you have to have an enthusiasm for life. You have to have a dream, a goal. And you have to be willing to work for it."

—Jim Valvano, basketball

GOLF

"It took me seventeen years to get three thousand hits in baseball. I did it in one afternoon on the golf course."

—Hank Aaron, baseball

A GOOD CATCHER

"A good catcher is the quarterback, the carburetor, the lead dog, the pulse taker, the traffic cop, and sometimes a lot of unprintable things, but no team gets very far without one."

—Miller Huggins, baseball

GREATNESS

"No club that wins a pennant once is an outstanding club. One which bunches two pennants is a good club. But a team which can win three in a row really achieves greatness."

—Babe Ruth, baseball

"I can't believe that God put us on this earth to be ordinary."

—Lou Holtz, football

GREAT SOCIAL EXPERIMENTS

"Jackie, we've got no army. There's virtually nobody on our side. No owners, no umpires, very few newspapermen. And I'm afraid that many fans will be hostile. We'll be in a tough position. We can win only if we can convince the world that I'm doing this because you're a great ballplayer, a fine gentleman."

—Branch Rickey, baseball

GUTS

"Gold medals aren't really made of gold. They're made of sweat, determination, and a hard-to-find alloy called guts."

—Dan Gable, freestyle wrestling

HANDLING STRESS

"If you try to fight the course, it will beat you."

—Lou Holtz, football

"The key to winning is poise under stress."

—Paul Brown, football

HEART

"It is not the size of a man but the size of his heart that matters."

—Evander Holyfield, boxing

"Battles are primarily won in the hearts of men."

—Vince Lombardi, football

"A man not perfect, but of heart so high, of such heroic rage, that even his hopes became a part of earth's eternal heritage."

—Rick Pitino, basketball

HELL

"I'll put you through hell, but at the end of it all we'll be champions."

—Paul "Bear" Bryant, football

HOME-FIELD ADVANTAGE

"Yeah, RFK was a crummy stadium. We had crud hanging off it. The fans are right on top of everybody. When people came in there, it was hard to beat us."

—Joe Gibbs, football

"We use the same boys and the same plays on the road as we do at home. Our execution is expected to be the same. At home we're the hosts, and I never liked the idea of being embarrassed in front of our friends. On the road we're somebody's else's guests, and we play in a way that they're not going to forget we visited them."

—Knute Rockne, football

HONESTY

"I have a rule on my team: when we talk to one another, we look each other right in the eye, because I think it's tough to lie to somebody. You give respect to somebody."

—Mike Krzyzewski, basketball

"I motivate players through communication, being honest with them, giving them respect, and appreciating their ability and help."

—Tommy Lasorda, baseball

HONOR

"Success without honor is an unseasoned dish. It will satisfy your hunger, but it won't taste good."

—Joe Paterno, football

HOPE

"So, I close in saying that I may have had a tough break, but I have an awful lot to live for."

—Lou Gehrig, baseball (Gehrig was terminally ill when he gave his famous "Farewell Speech" at Yankee Stadium, Bronx, New York, July 4, 1939)

"Don't look back. Something might be gaining on you."

—Leroy "Satchel" Paige, baseball

HUMANITY

"Humanity is the keystone that holds nations and men together. When that collapses, the whole structure crumbles. This is as true of baseball teams as any other pursuit in life."

—Connie Mack, baseball

HUMAN SPIRIT

"Each warrior wants to leave the mark of his will, his signature, on important acts he touches. This is not the voice of ego but of the human spirit, rising up and declaring that it has something to contribute to the solution of the hardest problems, no matter how vexing!"

—Pat Riley, basketball

HUMILITY

"Right after the game, say as little as possible."

—Tom Landry, football

"Self-praise is for losers. Be a winner. Stand for something. Always have class, and be humble."

—John Madden, football

"It's what you learn after you know it all that counts."

—John Wooden, basketball

HUMOR

"The problem with having a sense of humor is often that people you use it on aren't in a very good mood."

—Lou Holtz, football

HUSTLE

"I've got a theory that if you give 100 percent all of the time, somehow things will work out in the end. Push yourself again and again. Don't give an inch until the final buzzer sounds."

—Larry Bird, basketball

ILLNESS

"If your stomach disputes you, lie down and pacify it with cool thoughts."

—Leroy "Satchel" Paige, baseball

IMAGINATION

"The man who has no imagination has no wings."

—Muhammad Ali, boxing

"Imagination has a great deal to do with winning."

—Mike Krzyzewski, basketball

INDEPENDENCE

"Encourage members of your team to take the initiative and act on their own."

—Mike Krzyzewski, basketball

"A great player must rise to the occasion and turn the game around on his own."

—Joe Paterno, football

INDIVIDUAL EFFORT

"You never win a game unless you beat the guy in front of you. The score on the board doesn't mean a thing. That's for the fans. You've got to win the war with the man in front of you. You've got to get your man."

—Vince Lombardi, football

INDIVIDUALITY

"We have got great individuals but this team is not about individuals."

—David Beckham, soccer

"You don't have to be Magic to be special. You're already special, you're you."

—Earvin "Magic" Johnson, basketball

"When someone tells me there is only one way to do things, it always lights a fire under my butt. My instant reaction is, I'm gonna prove you wrong."

—Picabo Street, downhill skiing

INJURY

"Every time that happens, it's an opportunity for the next person. . . . We prepare hard. We come to the game with forty-five guys, and everyone needs to be ready to go. It's tough to lose those guys at the beginning of the game, but the players played competitively and the team played competitively. Unfortunately, it's part of the game."

—Bill Belichick, football

"I managed to make something for myself racing here. Although I never won any titles I really felt like I belonged.

I enjoyed my time. I just loved it more than anything else in the world. To those top guys out there, if you think your bike's not running well, it's a hard day, you know it's raining, I shouldn't get up and go racing, that's not hard, mate. Getting up in the morning and taking two hours to get changed, have a shower, and go to the toilet, that's hard. So if you ever need some motivation to go training or to chase your dreams, that's what it's like. If someone walked up to me and offered me a KLX110 and paid me five bucks to turn up on the startline, man, I'd do that. I'd give anything to have that again. I guess that's all I can say is to chase your dreams and go after it because I still do that. I've got a dream to race go-karts and, damn, I might get that Australian title that I was searching for in Motocross."

—Niki Urwin, motocross (speaking for the first time after a paralyzing crash)

"When you talk about an injury and the kind of depression you go through, it's not just because you're out of shape and you can't go out and play. You're missing a part of you. That's what's painful. That's what hurts."

—Jamila Wideman, basketball

INNOVATION

"A successful leader has to be innovative. If you are not one step ahead of the crowd, you'll soon be a step behind everyone else."

—Tom Landry, football

INSIDE-OUT COMPLIMENT

"He's not very fast, but maybe Elizabeth Taylor can't sing."

—Darrell Royal, football

INTEGRITY

"To be a successful coach, you should be and look prepared. You must be a man of integrity. Never break your word. Don't have two sets of standards. Remember, you don't handle players—you handle pets. You deal with players. Stand up for your players. Show them you care—on and off the court."

—Red Auerbach, basketball

INTELLIGENCE

"Slow thinkers are part of the game too. Some of these slow thinkers can hit a ball a long way."

—Alvin Dark, baseball

"Finish last in your league and they call you idiot. Finish last in medical school and they call you doctor."

—Abe Lemons, basketball

INTIMIDATION

"Every great batter works on the theory that the pitcher is more afraid of him than he is of the pitcher."

—Ty Cobb, baseball

"You have to defeat a great player's aura more than his game."

—Pat Riley, basketball

JOB SECURITY

"There's pressure on me. There's pressure on our whole football team. I'm not one of those guys that's trying to hang on to a job. If I'm not good enough to get things done, I shouldn't be here. And I will never waver from that. I know some guys that will do anything to stay here or play here or do whatever. Hey man, be honest with yourself. Because you have to look at yourself in the mirror and say, 'Am I good enough or not good enough?' That's the way it is. I've been a coach long enough to realize the nature of this business and what you have to do. I know a lot of things have happened the past few years. I know the fan base is really upset with the way we've played, and they should be."

—Ray Rhodes, football

JUSTICE

"In this game of baseball, you live by the sword and die by it. You hit and get hit. Remember that."

—Alvin Dark, baseball

LAZINESS

"One thing I never want to be accused of is not working."

—Don Shula, football

LEADERSHIP

"Leaders have to search for the heart on a team, because the person who has it can bring out the best in everybody else."

—Mike Krzyzewski, basketball

"Leadership is getting someone to do what they don't want to do, to achieve what they want to achieve. It is a matter of having people look at you and gain confidence, seeing how you react. If you're in control, they're in control."

—Tom Landry, football

"Leaders aren't born, they are made. And they are made just like anything else, through hard work. And that's the price we'll have to pay to achieve that goal, or any goal."

—Vince Lombardi, football

"Remember this, son. One percent of ballplayers are leaders of men. The other 99 percent are followers of women."

—John McGraw, baseball

"You can't lead anyone else further than you have gone yourself."

—Gene Mauch, baseball

"We need people who influence their peers and can't be detoured from their convictions by their peers that don't have any convictions."

—Joe Paterno, football

"Leadership, like coaching, is fighting for the hearts and souls of men and getting them to believe in you."

—Eddie Robinson, football

"I don't know any other way to lead but by example."

—Don Shula, football

LEARNING

"I learn teaching from teachers. I learn golf from golfers. I learn winning from coaches."

—Harvey Penick, golf

LEARNING FROM DEFEAT

"I cannot get rid of the hurt from losing, but after the last out of every loss, I must accept that there will be a tomorrow. In fact, it's more than there'll be a tomorrow, it's that I want there to be a tomorrow. That's the big difference. I want tomorrow to come."

—Sparky Anderson, baseball

"I am not happy with moral victories. Those are forgotten. If I take a bad licking, I can't wait to get it straightened out. What did I do wrong? How can I change this? How can we turn this ship around? That's the whole motivational thing in coaching."

—Bobby Bowden, football

"You can learn a line from a win and a book from a defeat."

—Paul Brown, football

"Losing doesn't make me want to quit. It makes me want to fight that much harder."

—Paul "Bear" Bryant, football

"Success is never permanent, and failure is never final."

—Mike Ditka, football

"I think everyone should experience defeat at least once during their career. You learn a lot from it."

—Lou Holtz, football

"I'm fortunate now that I coach at Duke University and we've won a lot. I have some kids who haven't failed that much. But when they get to college, they're going to fail some time. That's a thing that I can help them the most with."

—Mike Krzyzewski, basketball

"I've learned that something constructive comes from every defeat."

—Tom Landry, football

"About the only problem with success is that it does not teach you how to deal with failure."

—Tommy Lasorda, baseball

"You can't win them all."

—Connie Mack, baseball

"What you get from games you lose is extremely important. You have no choices about how you lose, but you do have a choice about how you come back and prepare to win again."

—Pat Riley, basketball

"It's hard to win a pennant, but it's harder to lose one."

—Chuck Tanner, baseball

PAUL BROWN

Paul Brown was born in Ohio in 1908, the son of a railroad worker and his wife. He was the star quarterback at Washington High School in Massillon, Ohio, immediately following in that role Harry Stuhldreher, who went on to become one of the Notre Dame Fighting Irish's famous "Four Horsemen." After attending Miami of Ohio, where he was also a football star, he went on to have a successful coaching career both at the high school and college levels. After coaching his old high school team he became the Ohio State Buckeyes head coach from 1941–1943. In 1944 he was commissioned as a lieutenant in the U.S. Navy where he spent the last two years of World War II. During that time he served at the Great Lakes Naval Station as head coach of the Navy's Bluejacket football team. But it was as a coach of professional football that he earned his greatest fame. He became the founder and owner of the Cleveland Browns, and one of the founding fathers of today's National Football League. He was the Browns' head coach from 1946–1962, and had a career record of 170-106-6. He took his team to the league championship six times, in 1947–1949 in the All-American Football Conference, and in 1950, 1954, and 1955 in the NFL. After leaving the Browns, he founded the Cincinnati Bengals in 1967 and became their first head coach. He is considered the "father of the modern offense" and one of the greatest pro football coaches ever. He died in 1991 at the age of 82.

"If you fail the first time that's just a chance to start over again."

—Lenny Wilkens, basketball

LEISURE

"Leisure time is that five or six hours when you sleep at night."

—George Allen, football

LIFE

"Don't go to the grave with life unused."

—Bobby Bowden, football

"You can never pay back, but you can always pay forward."

—Woody Hayes, football

"Life is 10 percent what happens to you and 90 percent how you respond to it."

—Lou Holtz, football

"It's a mere moment in a man's life between the all-star game and an old-timer's game."

—Vin Scully, baseball

"If all I'm remembered for is being a good basketball player, then I've done a bad job with the rest of my life."

—Isiah Thomas, basketball

LIMITATIONS

"People ask me if I could fly. I said, 'Yeah, for a little while.'"

—Michael Jordan, basketball

THE LOAD

"It's not the load that breaks you down, it's the way you carry it."

—Lou Holtz, football

LOSING

"Every time you win, you're reborn. When you lose, you die a little."

—George Allen, football

"If the day ever comes when I can swallow defeat, I'll quit."

—Toe Blake, hockey

"The winning doesn't feel as good as the losing does bad."

—Bobby Bowden, football

"If a tie is like kissing your sister, losing is like kissing your grandmother with her teeth out!"

—George Brett, baseball

LOVE

"I just love to coach. That may sound simple, but I think sometimes people like the things that go around coaching and not the actual job. I have always gotten my greatest pleasure out of breaking down film, learning about opponents and yourself, then implementing a game plan to take advantage of your strengths and their weaknesses. I love to take a group of young men in the late summer and mold them into a team."

—Bobby Bowden, football

"Love is the force that ignites the spirit and binds teams together."

—Phil Jackson, basketball

"Guys ask me, don't I get burned out? How can you get burned out doing something you love? I ask you, have you ever got tired of kissing a pretty girl?"

—Tommy Lasorda, baseball

"Teamwork is what the Green Bay Packers were all about. They didn't do it for individual glory. They did it because they loved one another."

—Vince Lombardi, football

"I love the young men that I coached."

—Rick Pitino, basketball

LOVING THE GAME

"Even when I'm old and gray, I won't be able to play it, but I'll still love the game."

—Michael Jordan, basketball

"Yeah, but I love you more than football and basketball."

—Tommy Lasorda, baseball (to his wife)

"There is but one game and that game is baseball."

—John McGraw, baseball

"No matter what I talk about, I always get back to baseball."

—Connie Mack, baseball

"Too few of us realize what we have in golf, a game that provides small miracles of pleasure almost from the cradle to the grave."

—Hugh McIlvanney, golf

"I can't remember a time in my life when I haven't hated football. Come on—anyone who paid attention to my career must have suspected it. When did I ever look like I was enjoying myself? When did you last see me smile on the sidelines or in the locker room? You must have at least wondered why I was always so angry with everyone around me. I'll tell you why—I was goddamn miserable. Football sucks. . . . All that pressure, having to deal with all those dumbass players, just to play a game that's basically a lot of choreographed shoving? . . . Solid-gold citizens, football players. If they're not boring as hell, they're arrogant drug-crazed felons."

—Bill Parcells, football

CONNIE MACK

Connie Mack (1862–1956) was the longtime owner/manager of the Philadelphia Athletics. Because he both owned and managed the team, he could not be fired, and he stayed at the helm of his club long after he stopped remembering the names of the players. Baseball's rules now prohibit an owner from managing his own baseball team, so we will never see the likes of Connie Mack again. Despite a lifetime in baseball, Mack can never have his jersey number retired. When he played major league baseball, as a catcher, players didn't wear jersey numbers and, during the half century that he managed, he wore a business suit in the dugout rather than his team's uniform, as is the custom. Mack sat in the dugout holding a scorebook, which he would wave to position his outfielders. He played for the Washington Nationals of the National League from 1886–1889, and for the Pittsburgh Pirates from 1891–1896. He managed the Pirates from 1894–1896, and managed the Philadelphia A's from 1901–1950. He was known, in his prime, as the Tall Tactician. Mack's best team was the 1929 A's, featuring Jimmie Foxx, Mickey Cochrane, and Al Simmons swinging the bat, and Lefty Grove and George Earnshaw on the mound. They won 104 games, beat out the "Murderers' Row" New York Yankees to win the AL pennant, then beat the Cubs in the World Series. In 1949, the New York Yankees turned Old-Timers Day into a Mack tribute. He was 86 at the time. Asked to name his all-time Athletics team, he said, catcher Mickey Cochrane, first basemen Jimmy Foxx and Stuffy McInnis, second baseman Eddie Collins, third baseman Frank Baker, shortstop Jack Barry, outfielders Al Simmons and Mule Haas and Bing Miller, and pitcher Lefty Grove.

LUCK

"Today I consider myself the luckiest man on the face of the Earth."

—Lou Gehrig, baseball

"The man who complains about the way the ball bounces is likely the one who dropped it."

—Lou Holtz, football

"Football is a great game. It demands a young man's total commitment—emotionally, mentally, and physically. It challenges our young people to do their very best, to discipline themselves to develop mental, as well as physical, toughness. At its best, it is a wonderful and worthwhile experience, which will have immense future character benefits for its players."

—Joe Paterno, football

"The harder you work, the luckier you get."

—Gary Player, golf

"Luck is the residue of design."

—Branch Rickey, baseball

"When I'm driving to Yankee Stadium and back, I do it so often. I don't remember passing lights, I don't remember paying tolls, coming over the bridge. Going back over the bridge, I remember."

—Phil Rizzuto, baseball

"Breaks balance out. The sun don't shine on the same ol' dog's rear end every day. Luck is what happens when preparation meets opportunity. You've got to think lucky. If you fall into a mudhole, check your back pocket—you might have caught a fish."

—Darrell Royal, football

"Luck? Sure. But only after long practice and only with the ability to think under pressure."

—Mildred "Babe" Didrikson Zaharias, golf

MAGIC

"When he shoots, it doesn't even look like he touches the puck."

—Al Arbour, hockey (about Mike Bossy)

BABE DIDRICKSON ZAHARIAS

One of the great female athletes of all time, Babe was born in Texas in 1911. She first made news with her athleticism as an All-American high-school basketball player. At age 21 she won several events at the Amateur Athletic Union track-and-field meet. In that year's Summer Olympics she won gold medals in the javelin and 80-meter hurdles. She began her career in golf, the sport for which she is best remembered, in 1934. She won 31 tournaments, including ten majors. She also excelled at, among other things, tennis, diving, billiards, archery, roller-skating, bowling, and swimming. She was once asked if there was anything she didn't play. "Yeah, dolls," she said. She died in 1956 of cancer.

MAKING MISTAKES

"Football is a game of errors. The team that makes the fewest errors in a game usually wins."

—Paul Brown, football

"Failure is good. It's fertilizer. Everything I've learned about coaching, I've learned from making mistakes."

—Rick Pitino, basketball

AL ARBOUR

Al Arbour was born in 1932 in Sudbury, Ontario, Canada. He made his debut as an NHL hockey player in 1953, as a defenseman for the Detroit Red Wings. He was on three Stanley Cup teams: the Red Wings, the Chicago Black Hawks in 1961, and the Toronto Maple Leafs in 1963 and 1964. He also played for the St. Louis Blues before retiring after the 1970–1971 season. He was the last NHL player to play while wearing eyeglasses. He was twice named to the NHL All-Star team. His greatest years as an NHL coach, however, began in 1973 when he took the helm for the New York Islanders. He led the Isles to four straight Stanley Cups (1980–1983) and five consecutive first-place finishes in the Patrick Division. He retired as a coach in 1986—with a career record of 739-537-223 during the regular season and 119-79 in the playoffs—to join the Islanders' front office. Arbour won the 1992 Lester Patrick Award for outstanding service to hockey in the United States. Arbour still has the record for most NHL games as a player and coach (2,227) and is second all-time in games coached (1,606), career victories (781), playoff games (209), playoff wins (123) and playoff series wins (30). He was inducted as a member of the Hockey Hall of Fame in 1996. Upon his retirement as Islanders' coach, Arbour had been at the helm for 1,499 games. On November 3, 2007, the Islanders brought Arbour back for one game so that, at age 75, he could reach the 1,500-game milestone.

"I try not to make the same mistakes today that I made yesterday."

—Darrell Royal, football

"If you're not making mistakes, then you're not doing anything. I'm positive that a doer makes mistakes."

—John Wooden, basketball

MANAGEMENT

"Management must speak with one voice. When it doesn't, management itself becomes a peripheral opponent to the team's mission."

—Pat Riley, basketball

MATURITY

"You got to be a man to play baseball for a living, but you got to have a lot of little boy in you, too."

—Roy Campanella, baseball

MENTAL HEALTH

"They call me eccentric. They used to call me nuts. I haven't changed."

—Al McGuire, basketball

MENTAL TOUGHNESS

"What makes you really come together under pressure is determination and focus and toughness."

—Debi Thomas, figure skating

"Mental toughness is to physical as four is to one."

—Bobby Knight, basketball

"Mental toughness is essential to success. Its qualities are sacrifice and self-denial. Also, most importantly, it is combined with a perfectly disciplined will that refuses to give in. It's a state of mind—you could call it character in action."

—Vince Lombardi, football

"Don't let what you cannot do interfere with what you can do."

—John Wooden, basketball

MIRACLES

"Ingenuity plus courage plus work equals miracles."

—Bob Richards, track and field

MISERY

"There is winning and there is misery."

—Bill Parcells, football

MISTAKES

"Eliminate the mistakes and you'll never lose a game. To eliminate mistakes, you have to pick the right QB. And the pass is a weapon of surprise—don't overuse it."

—Woody Hayes, football

"What to do with a mistake—recognize it, admit it, learn from it, forget it."

—Dean Smith, basketball

"Most ball games are lost, not won."

—Casey Stengel, baseball

MONEY

"I'd learned how much happiness money can bring you. Very little."

—Rick Pitino, basketball

MORALE

"A coach does not have to concern himself with how a first stringer feels. The real test is whether the last substitute has good morale. If he has, it means everyone has."

—Joe Paterno, football

MOTIVATION

"It's kind of interesting as to what motivates people, because everybody is motivated by something. Mine has always been the motivation of fear. I coach as hard as I can in order to keep from losing. When we lose a game, it hurts many more times more than a win feels good. When you win a ball game, twenty-four hours and it's over. When you lose, it dwells with you for years. You wonder, could I have done this or that differently?"

—Bobby Bowden, football

"The ones who want to achieve and win championships motivate themselves."

—Mike Ditka, football

"To succeed you need to find something to hold on to, something to motivate you, something to inspire you."

—Tony Dorsett, football

"Motivation is simple. You eliminate those who are not motivated."

—Lou Holtz, football

"I don't believe in team motivation. I believe in getting a team prepared . . . If you are prepared, you will be confident, and will do the job."

—Tom Landry, football

"The only way to get people to like working hard is to motivate them. Today, people must understand why they're working hard. Every individual in an organization is motivated by something different."

—Rick Pitino, basketball

" There's always the motivation of wanting to win. Everybody has that. But a champion needs a motivation above and beyond winning."

—Pat Riley, basketball

"A team in an ordinary frame of mind will do only ordinary things. In the proper emotional state, a team will do extraordinary things. To reach this state, a team must have a motive that has an extraordinary appeal to them."

—Knute Rockne, football

"Praise is a great motivator. Criticism is a great teaching tool if done properly, but praise is the best motivator."

—John Wooden, basketball

MYSTICAL ANALOGIES

"An acre of performance is worth a whole world of promise."

—Red Auerbach, basketball

"A bird doesn't sing because it has an answer, it sings because it has a song."

—Lou Holtz, football (quoting Maya Angelon)

TOMMY LASORDA

Tommy Lasorda (born in 1927) was manager of the Los Angeles Dodgers for twenty years, leading his team to eight division titles, four pennants, and two world championships (1981, 1988). As a player, manager, and front-office executive, he has spent more than fifty years with the Dodger organization. In 2000 he led the U.S. baseball team to an Olympic gold metal. Today he remains a top spokesman and ambassador of good will for the game of baseball.

"Baseball is like driving, it's the one who gets home safely that counts."

—Tommy Lasorda, baseball

"If the waitress has dirty ankles, the chili should be good."

—Al McGuire, basketball

"Don't worry about the horse being blind, just load the wagon."

—John Madden, football

JOHN MADDEN

John Madden is today best known as the color commentator for NBC's Sunday Night football and the guy with his own video game. But before moving up to the TV booth, he was the Super Bowl–winning head coach of the Oakland Raiders.

Madden was born in 1936 in Minnesota. Although he was drafted out of college by the Philadelphia Eagles, he never actually played pro football because of a pre-season knee injury. He began his coaching career in 1960 with five seasons at a junior college in California, then three more at San Diego State. He became an assistant coach for the Oakland Raiders in 1967, became head coach for that team in 1969, and held that position until 1978 when he retired because of stomach problems. The highlight of his coaching career came when his Raiders won Super Bowl XI in 1977, defeating the Minnesota Vikings by a score of 32-14.

His career record as an NFL coach is 105-32-7, giving him the best winning percentage of any pro coach ever. (Second place belongs to Vince Lombardi, who was 105-35-6.) In 1980 he began a second career in TV, and has worked for CBS, Fox, and NBC. He is known for his onomatopoeic exclamations ("Boom!") while describing football plays. He has earned 13 Emmys—the award for television excellence—for his color commentary.

His video game, Madden Football, is one of the most popular ever sold. In addition to analyzing football games for TV broadcasts, Madden has also made many TV commercials and has written several books. Because of his fear of flying, Madden travels from city to city between games in a customized bus known as the Madden Cruiser.

"You can lead a horse to water, but you can't stick his head in it."

—Paul Owens, baseball

"An automobile goes nowhere efficiently, unless it has a quick, hot spark to ignite things, to set the cogs of the machine in motion. So I try to make every player on my team feel he's the spark keeping our machine in motion. On him depends our success and victories."

—Knute Rockne, football

"If worms carried pistols, birds wouldn't eat 'em."

—Darrell Royal, football

NEGATIVITY

"If you burn your neighbor's house down, it doesn't make your house look any better."

—Lou Holtz, football

"I just don't deal with the negativity. I can't get involved in that side of it. I don't understand it, and you can't let it take away from your life and what you are trying to do."

—Rick Pitino, basketball

"My responsibility is leadership, and the minute I get negative, that is going to have an influence on my team."

—Don Shula, football

9/11

"We realized that in spite of all the sadness and devastation, people were looking to us for, I wouldn't say relief, but a distraction, a support system. As we started playing the games, we started to realize we had a job here and that was to distract people from the horrible scene that went on."

—Joe Torre, baseball

NOISE

"I like a noisy ball club. In fact, I insist upon it. A team that is making a lot of noise is on its toes and hustling. It suggests that you want to win, have plenty of pep and ginger."

—Connie Mack, baseball

THE NORTH SIDE

"Every player should be accorded the privilege of at least one season with the Chicago Cubs. That's baseball as it should be played—in God's own sunshine. And that's really living."

—Alvin Dark, baseball

NOSTALGIA

"You look forward to Opening Day like a birthday party when you're a kid. You think something wonderful is going to happen."

—Joe DiMaggio, baseball

"When you coach as long as I did, you can't help but miss those Saturdays—dealing with the players, the game preparation, the challenges, the excitement."

—Tom Osborne, football

NUTRITION

"We went inside and watched *Hoosiers* for about thirty minutes, and told the kids to just get relaxed. We fed them some fruit and peanut butter, and then came back out and played well."

—Tom Osborne, football

OBSESSION

"Baseball and malaria keep coming back."

—Gene Mauch, baseball

"To have long-term success as a coach or in any position of leadership, you have to be obsessed in some way."

—Pat Riley, basketball

OBSTACLES

"I had an incredible experience living in New York, playing for the Yankees, to go through all of the things I did, including the no-hitter. It was a very memorable time. I love the game. I can honestly say that having a uniform on feels comfortable to me, being at the ballpark feels like home, so I'd like to be involved with the game in some capacity. I still have young kids, and my priority is at home right now, but maybe eventually I'll find the right situation to be involved in some capacity. I loved throwing a baseball. It is so important to find something in life you feel crazy about. Because you are so passionate you naturally practice. The hard work that it takes to do something well will come easily. I still get a lot of letters from kids and parents who face different challenges and disabilities. I share some of the lessons that I learned through sports and baseball, which makes me feel good. It's incredible to have an impact that way. I worked very hard. I felt I could play the game. The only thing that could stop me was myself."

—Jim Abbott, baseball

JIM ABBOTT

Jim Abbott was born without a right hand, yet went on to pitch a no-hitter in the major leagues. A star pitcher for the University of Michigan, Jim never played a day of minor league ball, instead moving from campus directly to the majors. He won twelve games during his rookie year of 1989 with the Anaheim Angels. While pitching, he wore his glove over the end of his right arm. After releasing the ball he would almost instantaneously move the glove onto his left hand so that he would be in position to field the ball. And, if the ball was hit to him, once again using sleight of hand, he would move the glove back to his right arm, while retaining the ball in his hand so he could throw. Although his stats were fairly mediocre for his career, the obvious high point came in 1992 when, while pitching for the New York Yankees in Yankee Stadium, he pitched a no-hitter against the Cleveland Indians. Since retiring from baseball Jim has dedicated his life to inspiring others with so-called disabilities to make the most of their lives.

THE OFF-SEASON

"People ask me what I do in winter when there's no baseball. I'll tell you what I do. I stare out the window and wait for spring."

—Rogers Hornsby, baseball

ROGERS HORNSBY

Rogers Hornsby (1896–1963) was one of baseball's greatest hitters. When he retired he had the second highest lifetime batting average of all time (.358), trailing only Ty Cobb. Born and raised in rural Texas, he was a late bloomer. Although obsessed with baseball, he struggled in the minor leagues as a teenager and didn't turn into one of the greatest right-handed batters of all times until future Yankees manager Miller Huggins adjusted his stance and leveled out his swing. He was a major league rookie in 1915 for the Cardinals. On defense he could play just about anywhere, with the exception of pitcher and catcher. Known as "The Rajah," he played for the Cardinals from 1915–1926 (he served as both player and manager in 1925–1926), then for the Giants, Braves, and Cubs. As his playing career wore down, he functioned as both player and manager, this time for the Braves, then the Cubs for a few years. After retiring, he also managed the St. Louis Browns. He was married three times and could usually be found at the track when he wasn't at the ballpark. He was inducted into the Baseball Hall of Fame in his first year of eligibility in 1942. His .424 batting average in 1924 is the highest of the twentieth century.

ONE STEP AT A TIME

"The ideal way to win a championship is step by step."

—Phil Jackson, basketball

OPEN MIND

"The coach should be the absolute boss, but he still should maintain an open mind. Don't be so domineering that you want to show and prove that you're the boss every day. Do your job—but listen to people."

—Red Auerbach, basketball

"Each group and each youngster is different. As a leader or coach, you get to know what they need."

—Mike Krzyzewski, basketball

"Coaches have to watch for what they don't want to see and listen to what they don't want to hear."

—John Madden, football

OPPORTUNITY

"Great moments are born from great opportunity. And that's what you have here tonight, boys. That's what you've earned here, tonight. One game. If we played 'em ten times, they might win nine. But not this game. Not tonight. Tonight, we skate with them. Tonight, we stay with them, and we shut them down because we can! Tonight, we are the greatest hockey team in the world. You were born to be hockey players—every one of you. And you were meant to be here tonight. This is your time. Their time—is done. It's over. I'm sick and tired of hearing about what a great hockey team the Soviets have. Screw 'em! This is your time! Now go out there and take it!"

—Herb Brooks, hockey

"As long as I've got a chance to beat you I'm going to take it."

—Leo Durocher, baseball

HERB BROOKS

Herb Brooks is most famous as the coach of the 1980 "Do you believe in miracles?" U.S. Olympic hockey team that defeated the much-favored Soviet Union team in Lake Placid, New York, and went on to win the gold medal. After that memorable victory, Brooks coached in the National Hockey League, for the Minnesota North Stars (1987–1988), New Jersey Devils (1992–1993), Pittsburgh Penguins (1999–2000) and New York Rangers (1981–1985). He was born in St. Paul, Minnesota, and attended the University of Minnesota, where he played hockey. Twice he appeared in the Winter Olympics as a player in 1964 and 1968. He later coached the Gophers hockey team from 1972–1979, winning the national title three times. Sadly, Herb was killed at age 66 in a one-car accident in Minnesota in 2003.

"They said playing basketball would kill me. Well, not playing basketball was killing me."

—Earvin "Magic" Johnson, basketball

"When you cleanse yourself of a big victory, you may open yourself up to the opportunity for an even bigger victory."

—Mike Krzyzewski, basketball

"When a player gets injured, it's a big blow to the team. At the same time, it allows other people to step up, take on new roles."

—John Madden, football

"Do you know what my favorite part of the game is? The opportunity to play."

—Mike Singletary, football

"The American dream, to me, means having the opportunity to achieve, because I don't think you should be guaranteed anything other than opportunity."

—Lenny Wilkens, basketball

ORGANIZATION

"I've got a checklist for everything."

—Joe Paterno, football

OVER-COACHING

"Over-coaching is the worst thing you can do to a player."

—Dean Smith, basketball

OVER-CONFIDENCE

"There is nothing so uncertain as a sure thing."

—Scotty Bowman, hockey

"The minute you think you've got it made, disaster is just around the corner."

—Joe Paterno, football

"If we're going to win the pennant, we've got to start thinking we're not as good as we think we are."

—Casey Stengel, baseball

OVERTHINKING

"My theory of hitting was just to watch the ball as it came in and hit it."

—Tommy Lasorda, baseball

PAIN

"Pain is only temporary, no matter how long it lasts."

—Ray Lewis, football

PARENTS

"When you have a father and a mother who work all their lives so you can have an education and build your body—it's a blessing."

—Lou Gehrig, baseball

"Treat each player as your son or daughter, if you can. The parents have invested in you."

—Hank Iba, basketball

"My heroes are and were my parents. I can't see having anyone else as my heroes."

—Michael Jordan, basketball

"Most of all, I count the blessings of my family. Imagine how lucky I am to call the man whose memories I revere to this day by so many important names—teacher, coach, manager, and especially Dad. He was for me and many others an example of how to play and prepare for the game the right way—the Cal Sr. way. And alongside him there was always my mom, who to this day shines as an example of devotion to family and community, humility, integrity and love. Mom, the words are hard to find how much I love you back."

—Cal Ripken, Jr., baseball

"My father gave me the greatest gift anyone could give another person. He believed in me."

—Jim Valvano, basketball

PASSION

"I define passion as extreme emotion. When you are passionate, you always have your destination in sight and you are not distracted by obstacles. Because you love what you are pursuing, things like rejection and setbacks will not hinder you in your pursuit. You believe that nothing can stop you!"

—Mike Krzyzewski, basketball

THE PAST

"I don't live in the past. I'm a student of the past, and I try to learn from the past, although some people will say, 'You haven't done a very good job of it.' But for me to live in the past? Hell, no."

—Woody Hayes, football

PATIENCE

"We want to win immediately. To say you're building is an incomplete sentence. You're building for a future coach and general manager."

—Marv Levy, football

PATRIOTISM

"When this thing is all over, the whole world is going to know you guys. You want to know why? Because you are coming to play your hearts out. You are coming for one thing, to bring the gold medal to the United States, where it belongs in baseball. Baseball is our game and we cannot let these teams beat us. When you come here, you do not represent your family, nor the school you went to, or the town you come from, or the organization that signed you. You represent the United States of America, and you're going to do everything you can to make the United States proud of you and you're not going to do anything over here to embarrass our country."

—Tommy Lasorda, Olympic baseball manager

PERFECTION

"If you don't have time to do it right, when will you have time to do it over?"

—John Wooden, basketball

PERFORMANCE

"What you do should speak so loudly that no one can hear what you say."

—Marv Levy, football

"You have to perform at a consistently higher level than others. That's the mark of a true professional."

—Joe Paterno, football

PERSEVERENCE

"My motto was always to keep swinging. Whether I was in a slump or feeling badly having trouble off the field, the only thing to do was keep swinging."

—Hank Aaron, baseball

"Stick with it. Life is full of ups and downs and how we respond to adversity makes us who we are. You may have seen the highlights, the good times in my career, but there were many difficult times."

—Jim Abbott, baseball

"One of the most difficult things everyone has to learn is that for your entire life you must keep fighting and adjusting if you hope to survive. No matter who you are or what your position is you must keep fighting for whatever it is you desire to achieve."

—George Allen, football

"It ain't over till it's over."

—Yogi Berra, baseball

"Never quit. It is the easiest cop-out in the world. Set a goal and don't quit until you attain it. When you do attain it, set another goal, and don't quit until you reach it. Never quit."

—Paul "Bear" Bryant, football

"You're never a loser until you quit trying."

—Mike Ditka, football

"A race is not well-run unless you've crossed the finish line knowing that you couldn't have kept going for one more step. If you could have, then you didn't give it everything you had."

—Jackie Dugall, track and field

"You don't get hurt running straight ahead . . . three-yards-and-a-cloud-of-dust offense. I will pound you and pound you until you quit."

—Woody Hayes, football

"It's not the load that breaks you down—it's the way you carry it."

—Lou Holtz, football

"If you're trying to achieve, there will be roadblocks. I've had them; everybody has had them. But obstacles don't have to stop you. If you run into a wall, don't turn around and give up. Figure out how to climb it, go through it, or work around it."

—Michael Jordan, basketball

"I want a persistent player, not the consistent player. I want a team that is persistent, unyielding, enduring, staying with something despite obstacles."

—Bobby Knight, basketball

"A winner never stops trying."

—Tom Landry, football

"People striving, being knocked down and coming back, that's what builds character."

—Tom Landry, football

"Winners never quit and quitters never win."

—Vince Lombardi, football

"The only way to overcome is to hang in. Even I'm starting to believe that."

—Dan O'Brien, track and field (decathlete)

"Perseverance isn't just the willingness to work hard. It's that, plus the willingness to be stubborn about your own belief in yourself."

—Merlin Olsen, football

"Difficulties in life are intended to make us better, not bitter."

—Dan Reeves, football

"It may sound strange, but many champions are made champions by setbacks."

—Bob Richards, track and field (pole vault/decathlon)

"The will to win, the desire to succeed, the urge to reach your full potential. . . . "

—Eddie Robinson, football

"You have to go broke three times to learn how to make a living."

—Casey Stengel, baseball

"If you can't go through it, find a way around it. Don't spend all your time banging your head against that."

—Lenny Wilkens, basketball

"There's no great fun, satisfaction, or joy from doing something that's easy."

—John Wooden, basketball

PERSISTENCE

"Paralyze resistance with persistence."

—Woody Hayes, football

PERSPECTIVE

"It's just a job. Grass grows, birds fly, waves pound the sand. I beat people up."

—Muhammad Ali, boxing

"You win some, lose some, and wreck some."

—Dale Earnhardt, auto racing

"I am in boxing but not of boxing."

—Eddie Futch, boxing

"You're never as good as everyone tells you when you win, and you're never as bad as they say when you lose."

—Lou Holtz, football

"My boy, one small breeze doesn't make a windstorm."

—John McGraw, baseball

"Winning is overrated. The only time it is really important is in surgery and war."

—Al McGuire, basketball

"When you are younger you get blamed for crimes you never committed and when you're older you begin to get credit for virtues you never possessed. It evens itself out."

—Casey Stengel, baseball

"It's so important to know where you are."

—Jim Valvano, basketball

AL McGUIRE

McGuire was a New York City boy who, along with his brother Dick, were basketball stars in the Big Apple on both the college and pro levels. Al was selected by New York in the 1951 NBA draft and played as a Knick from 1951–1954. He was traded to Baltimore with Connie Simmons for Ray Felix and Chuck Grigsby during July 1954. He finished his NBA career with ten games for Baltimore in 1954–1955. He appeared in twenty-four Knicks playoff games in 1952, 1953, and 1954. He averaged four points per game as a Knick during the regular season and 3.5 in the playoffs. He graduated from St. John's Preparatory School in Brooklyn in 1947 before going to St. John's University in Queens. He played basketball all four of his years at St. John's, and as a senior was captain of the team that finished 26-5 and came in third place in the NIT. After his playing career was through, Al had a highly successful career as a college coach, peaking with a national championship at Marquette in 1977. He was an assistant coach at Dartmouth College in Hanover, New Hampshire, from 1955–1957, head coach at Belmont Abbey College in Belmont, North Carolina, from 1957–1964, and head coach at Marquette University in Milwaukee, Wisconsin, from 1964–1977. He also led Marquette to an NIT championship in 1970 and was the Associated Press, United Press International, and United States Basketball Writers Association Coach of the Year in 1971, the year Marquette finished the season with a won-loss record of 28-1. Although his teams had great success, he was perhaps most proud of the fact that while at Marquette 92 percent of his kids graduated.

Twenty-six of his players went on to play in the NBA. He was also Marquette's athletic director from 1973–1977. He was inducted into the Basketball Hall of Fame in 1992. He worked as a basketball announcer right up until his death in 2001. He appeared posthumously in an ESPN commercial advertising their coverage of the upcoming NCAA Tournament. In a physical manifestation of March Madness, Al portrayed the Mayor of Bracketsville. Al's son, Allie, was a star player at Marquette under his dad, and also had a cup of coffee with the Knicks. Al died of leukemia at age 72.

"I always tried to make clear that basketball is not the ultimate. It is of small importance in comparison to the total life we live. There is only one kind of life that truly wins, and that is the one that places faith in the hands of the Savior. Until that is done, we are on an aimless course that runs in circles and goes nowhere."

—John Wooden, basketball

PHILOSOPHY

"My pitching philosophy is simple—keep the ball away from the bat."

—Leroy "Satchel" Paige, baseball

POIGNANT PROVERBS

"Baseball is like church. Many attend, few understand."

—Leo Durocher, baseball

"When all is said and done, more is said than done."

—Lou Holtz, football

POPULARITY

"I'm not trying to win a popularity poll. I'm trying to win football games. I don't like nice people. I like tough, honest people."

—Woody Hayes, football

"No matter how much you've won, no matter how many games, no matter how many championships, no matter how many Super Bowls, you're not winning now, so you stink."

—Bill Parcells, football

POTENTIAL

"Each of us has been put on earth with the ability to do something well. We cheat ourselves and the world if we don't use that ability as best we can."

—George Allen, football

"Don't rate potential over performance."

—Jim Fassel, football

"The power of the human will to compete and the drive to excel beyond the body's normal capabilities is most beautifully demonstrated in the arena of sport."

—Aimee Mullins, track and field

"Well, that's baseball. Rags to riches one day and riches to rags the next. But I've been in it thirty-six years and I'm used to it."

—Casey Stengel, baseball

PRACTICE

"Winning is the science of being totally prepared."

—George Allen, football

"To give yourself the best possible chance of playing to your potential, you must prepare for every eventuality. That means practice."

—Seve Ballesteros, golf

"First master the fundamentals. When I was young, I never wanted to leave the court until I got things exactly correct. My dream was to become a pro. I don't know if I practiced more than anybody, but I sure practiced enough. I still wonder if somebody—somewhere—was practicing more than me."

—Larry Bird, basketball

"It's not the will to win, but the will to prepare to win that makes the difference."

—Paul "Bear" Bryant, football

"Good, better, best. Never let it rest. Until your good is better and your better is best."

—Tim Duncan, basketball

"Don't do anything in practice that you wouldn't do in the game."

—George Halas, football

"You might not be able to out-think, out-market or out-spend your competition, but you can out-work them"

—Lou Holtz, football

"BEAR" BRYANT

Paul William "Bear" Bryant (September 11, 1913–January 26, 1983) was the longtime head football coach of the Crimson Tide of the University of Alabama. Bryant, the penultimate of twelve children, was born to a farmer and his wife in Moro Bottom, Arkansas. According to legend he earned his nickname when he was thirteen and volunteered to wrestle a caged bear at a theater promotion. He played football in high school and his team won the Alabama state championship when he was a senior. He went to the University of Alabama and played end for the 1934 national championship team. His first coaching job was in 1936 at Union College in Jackson, Tennessee. He spent four years as an assistant coach at Alabama, one year as head coach at the University of Maryland, and eight seasons running the University of Kentucky program. His best season at Kentucky was 1950, concluding with a victory over Bud Wilkinson's number-one-ranked Oklahoma Sooners in the Sugar Bowl. In 1954 Bryant became head coach at Texas A&M University. In 1956, only two years after a dismal 1-9 first season, the team won the Southwest Conference championship with a 34-21 victory over the University of Texas at Austin. He returned to his *alma mater* as head coach at Alabama in 1958. It would be a job he'd hold for 25 years, winning six national titles (1961, 1964, 1965, 1973, 1978, and 1979). In 1971, Bryant installed the wishbone offense and changed college football forever. Bryant announced his retirement at the end of the 1982 season. His last game was a 21-15 victory in the Liberty Bowl in Memphis, Tennessee, over the University of Illinois.

"I never think that there's something I can't do, whether it's beating my opponent one on one or practicing another hour because something about my game is just not right."

—Earvin "Magic" Johnson, basketball

"The key is not the will to win . . . everybody has that. It is the will to prepare to win that is important. Everyone wants to be on a winning team, but no one wants to come to practice."

—Bobby Knight, basketball

"I don't believe in team motivation. I believe in getting a team prepared so it knows it will have the necessary confidence when it steps on a field and be prepared to play a good game. If you are prepared, you will be confident, and will do the job."

—Tom Landry, football

"It's not necessarily the amount of time you spend at practice that counts; it's what you put into practice that makes the difference."

—Eric Lindros, hockey

"There's no way running on a beach or at some high school playground that you're going to get in football shape like you do when you practice."

—Steve Mariucci, football

"The thrill isn't in the winning. It's in the doing."

—Chuck Noll, football

"Our players work so hard in practice, Saturdays seem easy by comparison."

—Joe Paterno, football

"You don't win by making sensational plays; you win by not making mistakes."

—Bum Phillips, football

"I don't count on the boy who waits till October, when it's cool and fun, then decides he wants to play."

—Darrell Royal, football

"It's hard to go out and practice every single day, and you get really tired. But you have to believe in yourself."

—Summer Sanders, swimming

"The difference between a good athlete and a top athlete is the top athlete will do the mundane things when nobody's looking."

—Susan True, gymnastics

"If you are ever going to achieve as much as you can in a sport, you are going to have to be willing to make a leap of faith to learn how much your body can handle."

—Meredith Rainey Valmon, track and field

"If you train hard, you'll not only be hard, you'll be hard to beat."

—Herschel Walker, football

"You play the way you practice. Practice the right way and you will play the right way."

—Pop Warner, football

"The will to prepare is the key ingredient to success."

—Bud Wilkinson, football

BUD WILKINSON

Charles Burnham "Bud" Wilkinson was born in 1916 in Minneapolis, Minnesota. After his mother died when he was seven, his father sent him to Shattuck Military Academy in Faribault, Minnesota, where he excelled in five sports. He attended the University of Minnesota and as quarterback of their football team led the Golden Gophers to three national championships. After college he worked for a time with his father's mortgage company and served in the navy aboard an aircraft carrier during World War II. After the war Wilkinson became the head coach of the University of Oklahoma Sooners football team. He held that job from 1947–1963 and led his team to three national championships (1950, 1955, and 1956) and fourteen conference championships. He amassed a record of 145-29-4 during those years, including a 47-game winning streak from 1953 to 1957, an NCAA Division I record that still stands. In 1964, he retired as a football coach at the young age of 47. Wilkinson ran as a Republican for the U.S. Senate in 1964 but lost in the Democratic landslide to Fred R. Harris. The following year Bud went into broadcasting and became color commentator for ABC's Saturday college football, working first with Chris Schenkel, and later Keith Jackson. In 1978, Wilkinson returned to coaching with the St. Louis Cardinals of the NFL. After two losing seasons, he was fired and returned to broadcasting. He was elected to the College Football Hall of Fame in 1969, and died in 1994 at the age of 77.

"It's the little details that are vital. Little things make big things happen."

—John Wooden, basketball

PRAISE

"You can motivate players better with kind words than you can with a whip."

—Bud Wilkinson, football

PREJUDICE

"Ethnic prejudice has no place in sports, and baseball must recognize the truth if it is to maintain stature as a national game."

—Branch Rickey, baseball

PRESET AGENDAS

"Approach the game with no preset agendas and you'll probably come away surprised at your overall efforts."

—Phil Jackson, basketball

PRESS RELATIONS

"The Lord taught me to love everybody, but the last ones I learned to love were the sportswriters."

—Alvin Dark, baseball

"What's the difference between a three-week old puppy and a sportswriter? In six weeks, the puppy stops whining."

—Mike Ditka, football

"All of us learn to write in the second grade. Most of us go on to greater things."

—Bobby Knight, basketball

PRESSURE

"When you are playing for a national championship, it's not a matter of life and death. It's more important than that."

—Duffy Daugherty, football

"Pressure is a word that is misused in our vocabulary. When you start thinking of pressure, it's because you've started to think of failure."

—Tommy Lasorda, baseball

"You shouldn't have to put the weight of the world on your shoulders every game. It should just happen."

—Louis Orr, basketball

"All right, this is it, the whole season coming down to just one ball game. Every mistake will be magnified. Every play will be magnified. And it's a tough night for the players. You stay awake, and you dream. And you think of what might be: if you are the hero or the goat."

—Phil Rizzuto, baseball

"If you make every game a life and death proposition, you're going to have problems. For one thing, you'll be dead a lot."

—Dean Smith, basketball

PRIDE

"Great champions have an enormous sense of pride. The people who excel are those who are driven to show the world and prove to themselves just how good they are."

—Nancy Lopez, golf

"Ain't no man can avoid being born average, but there ain't no man got to be common."

—Leroy "Satchel" Paige, baseball

"Losing a game is heartbreaking. Losing your sense of excellence or worth is a tragedy."

—Joe Paterno, football

"I don't care if I was a ditch-digger for a dollar a day, I'd want to do my job better than the fellow next to me. I'd want to be the best at whatever I do."

—Branch Rickey, baseball

PRIORITIES

"Once you agree on the price you and your family must pay for success, it enables you to ignore the minor hurts, the opponent's pressure, and the temporary failures."

—Vince Lombardi, football

"I think my top priority in life is to be a good husband and a good father. Then I hope to be a good influence on the young people with whom I come in contact to be a decent role model for them. I'd like to help them understand that values are important."

—Joe Paterno, football

"What you are as a person is far more important than what you are as a basketball player."

—John Wooden, basketball

PRIVILEDGE

"Some people are born on third base and go through life thinking they hit a triple."

—Barry Switzer, football

PROCRASTINATION

"If you wait, all that happens is that you get older."

—Mario Andretti, auto racing

PROGNOSTICATION

"I've never predicted anything. All I have ever said is that we will do the very best we can."

—Bobby Knight, basketball

"The game has kept faith with the public, maintaining its old admission price for nearly thirty years while other forms of entertainment have doubled and tripled in price. And it will probably never change."

—Connie Mack, baseball

PSYCHOLOGY

"Regardless of who was coaching them, they still would have been a great team. I said early in the season that they were the nicest, even sissiest bunch I ever had. I think they read it, because later on they got unfriendly."

—Paul "Bear" Bryant, football

PUBLICITY

"Publicity is like poison. It doesn't hurt unless you swallow it."

—Joe Paterno, football

QUITTING

"If you can accept defeat and open your pay envelope without feeling guilty, you're stealing."

—George Allen, football

"All quitters are good losers."

—Bob Zuppke, football

READING

"Never read print, it spoils one's eye for the ball."

—W. G. Grace, cricket

RECRUITING

"If I came in to recruit your son, I would tell you, your wife, and your son that I will be the most demanding coach your son can play for."

—Bobby Knight, basketball

"You have to go out and find the players, but they have to be good people. The football players are the most important people to me. I like being around them. I like teaching and seeing them succeed in life. That gives me the greatest thrill."

—Eddie Robinson, football

RELIGION

"There are three things important to every man in this locker room. His God, his family, and the Green Bay Packers. In that order."

—Vince Lombardi, football

REPUTATION

"Be more concerned with your character than your reputation, because your character is what you really are, while your reputation is merely what others think you are."

—John Wooden, basketball

RESILIENCY

"All of us get knocked down, but it's resiliency that really matters. All of us do well when things are going well, but the thing that distinguishes athletes is the ability to do well in times of great stress, urgency, and pressure."

—Roger Staubach, football

R-E-S-P-E-C-T

"Every one of our players respects every one of their players and their team as a whole. But once we cross that white line most of the respect will be out the window and we will be fighting to win the game."

—David Beckham, soccer

"If there is a mutual respect between players and coaches, that keeps the team honest and makes for a very healthy environment which in turn promotes other important qualities such as work ethic, integrity and a positive atmosphere for competing and winning."

—Jillian Ellis, soccer

"Leaders show respect for people by giving them time."

—Mike Krzyzewski, basketball

"I think that you have to communicate with people, and I think that respect is a two-way street."

—Lenny Wilkens, basketball

"The players' attitude toward you hinges on just one thing, and that is respect. If they do not respect you, you've lost them. If you have their respect, you've got it made."

—Bud Wilkinson, football

RESPONSIBILITY

"If anything goes bad, I did it. If anything goes semi-good, then we did it. If anything goes really good, then you did it. That's all it takes to get people to win football games."

—Paul "Bear" Bryant, football

"I'm a big believer that when you sign your name on a dotted line, there's more than just playing the game of baseball. There's a responsibility when you put on that uniform to the people who pay to go watch you play."

—Tony Gwynn, baseball

"Everybody wants to take responsibility when you win, but when you fail, all these fingers are pointing."

—Mike Krzyzewski, basketball

"The day you take complete responsibility for yourself, the day you stop making excuses, that's the day you start to the top."

—O.J. Simpson, football

RETALIATION

"You'll never get ahead of anyone as long as you try to get even with him."

—Lou Holtz, football

RETIREMENT

"I guess I'll retire someday if I live that long."

—Bobby Bowden, football

"Behind all the years of practice and all the hours of glory waits that inexorable terror of living without the game."

—Bill Bradley, basketball

"I can remember loving to recruit. I knew I was going to do my best. But traveling and recruiting doesn't appeal to me any more. It's not as much fun as it used to be. A few minutes ago,

I had a hard time getting through the lobby because of all the people. After today, that won't be happening."

—Paul "Bear" Bryant, football

"Old place-kickers never die, they just go on missing the point."

—Lou Groza, football

"It's just a few words, but those words encompassed our philosophy: 'Play hard; Play clean; Play to win! But win or lose you are still my guys.' I think that your chances of winning the next time out even after a loss are greater with that approach. It's been a long trip from the corner of 71st Street and Stony Island Avenue on the south side of Chicago to Canton, Ohio. It's taken me 76 years. But in the words of an old song, "I wouldn't have missed it for the world," because on every step of this joyous journey, I've been accompanied by some remarkable companions."

—Marv Levy, football

RIGHTS OF OTHERS

"Consider the rights of others before your own feelings, and the feelings of others before your own rights."

—John Wooden, basketball

BILL BRADLEY

Bradley was chosen by New York in the 1965 NBA draft and played his entire NBA career with the Knicks (1967–1977). Between being drafted and appearing as a Knick, Bill played a season for Olympia Simmenthal of the Italian League. As a Knick, he averaged 12.4 points per game. He appeared in eight consecutive playoffs, from 1968 until 1975, and played on the Knicks' two NBA championship teams. He was a 1973 All-Star and was inducted into the Pro Basketball Hall of Fame in 1983. Back home in Missouri, Bill—the son of a banker—was a star at Crystal City High School from 1957–1961. During his high school career he was a two-time All-State selection, three-time All-Conference selection and led his team into the Missouri State Final Four three times. He scored a total of 3,068 points and averaged 27.4 points per game in a 112-game high school career. He was recruited by more than seventy colleges and chose to go to Princeton where, after a year as a Rhodes Scholar, he became the College Player of the Year in 1965. He was a consensus First Team All-America in 1964 and 1965, First Team All-Academic in 1965, and led Princeton to the 1965 Final Four, where he scored a record 58 points against Wichita State. That performance earned him the tournament's Most Valuable Player award. At Princeton he scored more than thirty points per game over three seasons. He was a member of the gold medal–winning 1964 U.S. Olympic Team and a member of the World University Games U.S. Team in 1965. Bill received the Sullivan Award, presented to the top amateur athlete in the country in 1965. Bill got the nickname "Dollar Bill" from *New York Post* columnist Leonard Lewin. The writer called Bradley "Dollar Bill" after it was announced that Bradley had become the highest-paid Knick ever with a $125,000 contract. While still a Knick, Bradley wrote, "Although I play basketball for the money, and the amount of money is important, it is not the sole reason I play. The answer is not so easy to uncover. It lies much deeper in the workings of the game and in me." Following his basketball career, Bradley entered politics and became a powerful member of the Democratic Party. He served for eighteen years as the U.S. Senator from New Jersey. In 1992 he delivered the keynote speech at the Democratic National Convention which, appropriately enough, was held at Madison Square Garden that year. In 2000 he unsuccessfully ran for President. After politics, Bradley has enjoyed success as an author and on the lecture circuit. His Knicks Jersey Number 24 was retired by the Knicks and hung from the Garden rafters on February 18, 1984.

RISKS

"A great ballplayer is a player who will take a chance."

—Branch Rickey, baseball

THE ROAD

"The street to obscurity is paved with athletes who perform great feats before friendly crowds. Greatness in major league sports is the ability to win in a stadium filled with people who are pulling for you to lose."

—George Allen, football

ROLE MODELS

"Why do I have to be an example for your kid? You be an example for your own kid."

—Bob Gibson, baseball

"As the years passed, it became clear to me that kids see it all. Whether we like it or not, as big leaguers, we are role models. The only question is, will we be positive or will we be negative."

—Cal Ripken, Jr., baseball

RULES

"For the benefit of you younger fellows, we have a lot of rules on this club. Midnight curfew, stay out of the bar at the hotel where we're staying, wear a shirt and sweater to breakfast and a coat and tie to dinner. Think you can remember all that?"

—Hank Bauer, baseball

CAL RIPKEN, JR.

Cal Ripken, Jr.—born August 24, 1960, in Havre de Grace, Maryland—is best known for playing in a record 2,632 consecutive baseball games. The record included all of the games played by the Baltimore Orioles from May 30, 1982, until September 19, 1998, and broke the record previously held by the beloved New York Yankee first baseman Lou Gehrig. But, in addition to his luck (he never during that stretch suffered an injury that prevented him from playing), he was also a great ballplayer, and in 2007 he became a well-deserved member of the Baseball Hall of Fame.

During his major league career—1981–2001, all with the Orioles—Ripken whacked 3,184 hits and 431 home runs. For most of his career he was a Gold Glove–winning shortstop, although he moved to third base during the last few years of his career. Ripken was the American League's Rookie of the Year in 1982. He broke Gehrig's record in 1995 and that year was named by *Sports Illustrated* as Sportsman of the Year. After breaking the record, he said, "Tonight I stand here, overwhelmed, as my name is linked with the great and courageous Lou Gehrig. I'm truly humbled to have our names spoken in the same breath."

Since retiring from baseball, he has founded Ripken Baseball, a league for kids aged 12 and under, and the Aberdeen Ironbirds, a short-season Class A team in the New York–Pennsylvania League. His father, Cal Sr., was a manager in the Orioles farm system, and his younger brother Billy also played for the Orioles.

"The fewer rules a coach has, the fewer rules there are for players to break."

—John Madden, football

"The Ten Commandments were not a suggestion."

—Pat Riley, basketball

SACRIFICE

"The Tour de France is a daily festival of human suffering."

—Lance Armstrong, bicycle racing

"You only have twenty-seven outs and they are precious. I have no intention of giving away outs."

—Frank Robinson, baseball

SCHOOL SPIRIT

"I remember games when we were trying to get back from having lost, or maybe we lost a couple of games and the students sensed that we needed something a little bit extra, and they gave it to us."

—Bobby Knight, basketball

SECOND PLACE

"There is no room for second place. There is only one place in my game, and that's first place. I have finished second twice in my time at Green Bay, and I don't ever want to finish second again. There is a second-place bowl game, but it is a game for losers played by losers. It is and always has been an American zeal to be first in anything we do, and to win, and to win, and to win."

—Vince Lombardi, football

SECRET TO GOOD COACHING

"Inspiration can come from unexpected places. An old manager called—he told me that he didn't think I was finished. And that's all it took—we started working."

—Jim Abbott, baseball

"I can deal with anyone on any side of the track. You have to deal with everyone."

—Sparky Anderson, baseball

"In any good coach is the ability to communicate. In other words, a lot of coaches know their X's and O's, but the players must absorb it."

—Red Auerbach, basketball

"In the end, for me, it's more about having the best players that we can have on the roster. I think you have to look at it that way. You have to be cognizant of the overall makeup of your team, but you try and get the best players you can."

—Bill Belichick, football

"I can be tough if I have to. I just don't think yelling at players does any good. I'd rather take a guy over to the side quietly and tell him if he does something wrong."

—Yogi Berra, baseball

"Leadership is getting players to believe in you. If you tell a teammate you're ready to play as tough as you're able to, you'd better go out there and do it. Players will see right through a phony. And they can tell when you're not giving it all you've got. Leadership is diving for a loose ball, getting the crowd involved, getting other players involved. It's being able to take it as well as dish it out. That's the only way you're going to get respect from the players."

—Larry Bird, basketball

"A coach can't be concerned with the poor ballplayer. If the player can't make it, he's got to be out right away. It's a very tough aspect of coaching, and in this aspect I was weak. Some guys get fat on coaching, they get healthy and strong, but other guys get ulcers."

—Johnny Blood, football

"I am accountable for everything that goes on with this football team. I take that very personally. The buck stops here. I am accountable and am going to be the one that has to put us on a course to correct it."

—Brian Billick, football

"He who gets the best players usually wins."

—Bobby Bowden, football

"People think there are great mysteries connected with the game, but there are not. It's just teaching fundamentals."

—Paul Brown, football

"Don't do a lot of coaching just before the game. If you haven't coached them by fourteen minutes to two on Saturday, it's too late then."

—Paul "Bear" Bryant, football

"Coaching is preparation."

—Pete Carril, basketball

"A coach's most important job is evaluation of players."

—Lee Corso, football

"It's how well the average player performs that gives your team consistency and substance."

—Eddie Crowder, football

"A manager doesn't hear the cheers."

—Alvin Dark, baseball

"Either love your players or get out of coaching."

—Bobby Dodd, football

"Systems win! Believe in your system, and then sell it to your players."

—Billy Donovan, basketball

BILLY DONOVAN

Billy Donovan had quite a career at Providence under Coach Rick Pitino. He helped get the Friars to the Final Four and was named New England Player of the Year in 1987. He was inducted into the Providence Hall of Fame in 1999. Billy was signed by New York as a free agent on December 11, 1987. He played 44 Knicks games in 1987–1988, averaging 2.4 points per game. After basketball, Billy took a job on Wall Street for two years before getting a job as assistant coach at the University of Kentucky, once again under Pitino. After five years of training from the master, Billy was ready for a head coaching job of his own and landed the gig at Marshall University in West Virginia. After two years at Marshall, Billy was named head coach of the University of Florida Gators, a position he still holds. In 2006, Billy led the Gators to the NCAA championship, defeating UCLA 73–57 in the final game before 43,000 at the RCA Dome in Indianapolis, Indiana. Billy and his wife Christine have three children.

"Some people like to drive and harangue, but I just like to lead fighters to do what is necessary. Sometimes I can tell them something that will spur them on, but I don't depend on the muzzle philosophy of instruction. It's the content of the advice."

—Eddie Futch, boxing

"Never leave a field with a boy feeling you're mad at him. You can chew him out, but then pat him on the shoulder."

—Jake Gaither, football

"A successful coach needs a patient wife, loyal dog, and great quarterback—and not necessarily in that order."

—Bud Grant, football

"What makes a good coach? Complete dedication."

—George Halas, football

"Praise your kids. Inspire and motivate your players with praise. Ten years from now it won't matter what your record was. Will your kids love you or hate you?"

—Jim Harrick, basketball

"I don't apologize for anything. When I make a mistake, I take the blame and go on from there. I just despise to lose, and that has taken a man of mediocre ability and made a pretty good coach out of him."

—Woody Hayes, football

"I'm not buddy-buddy with the players. If they need a buddy, let them buy a dog."

—Whitey Herzog, baseball

"Coaches are like ducks. Calm on top, but paddling underneath. Believe me, there's a lot of leg movement."

—Ken Hitchcock, hockey

"If you don't demand that your people maintain high performances to remain on your team, why should they be proud of the association?"

—Lou Holtz, football

"A manager has his cards dealt to him and he must play them."

—Miller Huggins, baseball

"Treat a person as he is, and he will remain as he is. Treat him as he could be, and he will become what he should be."

—Jimmy Johnson, football

LOU HOLTZ

The eighth winningest head coach in college football history, Lou Holtz was born in 1937 in West Virginia. Though he only weighed 150 pounds he played linebacker at Kent State during the late 1950s. After college he worked as an assistant coach at several colleges before accepting his first head coaching job at William and Mary in 1969.

He led his team to a Southern Conference championship in 1970. He coached North Carolina State for four years before coaching the New York Jets for a year. In 1977, he returned to college coaching at Arkansas and spent seven years there, coaching in six bowl games.

He took over the head coaching job at the University of Minnesota in 1984. His next stop was at Notre Dame in 1986, where he coached until 1996. Holtz retired from coaching after the 1995 season and moved to the relatively stress-free world of television commentary.

But coaching was in his blood and he returned to the sidelines, this time at the University of South Carolina in 1999. This was a team in trouble, and they went 0-11 during his first campaign there. The following two seasons, however, things greatly improved (8-4 and 9-3) and those teams each finished their seasons with victories in the Outback Bowl. He remained at South Carolina through the 2004 season and returned to TV commentary. Since 2005 he has worked for ESPN.

During his coaching career, Holtz twice was named the National Coach of the Year (1977, 1988), was the SEC Coach of the Year in 2000, and the ACC Coach of the Year in 1972.

"Coaches who start listening to fans wind up sitting next to them."

—Johnny Kerr, basketball

"I would rather be thought of as a teacher than a coach."

—Bobby Knight, basketball

"A common mistake among those who work in sport is spending a disproportional amount of time on 'x's and o's' as compared to time spent learning about people."

—Mike Krzyzewski, basketball

"The secret to winning is constant, consistent management."

—Tom Landry, football

"The coach who thinks his coaching is more important than his players' talent is an idiot."

—Joe Lapchick, basketball

JOE LAPCHICK

Lapchick was born April 12, 1900, in Yonkers, New York, and died August 10, 1970. He coached the New York Knicks from 1947 until 1956, from the second year of the Basketball Association of America to the days of a well-established NBA. His only other coaching experience came in 1930–1931 when he directed the ABL's Cleveland Rosenblums. As an NBA coach, his team had a winning record for eight straight seasons. His overall record was 326-247 and he led the Knicks to the Eastern Division title in 1953 and 1954. The press loved him because they always knew where they could find him after a home game, the restaurant Leone's, and he was always good for a quote.

As a player he was just as influential—maybe more. He was the game's first big man who could also move. Up until Lapchick's time there had been some big guys playing, but to call them heavy-footed would have been an understatement. Inert was more like it. They were there to get in the way. Lapchick proved that a center (large for his time) could also be agile, and he became a pivot star. Joe didn't go to college and played basketball in whatever pro leagues were available to him in and around New York City. He sometimes played for more than one team during the same season. He played for the Holyoke Reds of the Interstate League in 1921–1922, the Schenectady Dorpians of the New York League in 1920–1922, the Troy Trojans from 1921–1923, the Brooklyn Visitations of the Metropolitan League from 1921–1923, the Toledo Red Men Tobaccos of the ABL in 1930–1931, the Cleveland Rosenblums of that same league from

1928–1931, where he won two league championships and was also player coach for a time, and the original Celtics, a team that played in a variety of leagues, off and on between 1923 and 1937.

Joe coached at the college level for St. John's from 1936–1947, and then again from 1957–1965. His overall record while coaching the Redmen was 334-130, for a phenomenal 72 percent winning percentage. He was at the helm when St. John's went to twelve NIT and one NCAA tournament. He was inducted into the Basketball Hall of Fame as a player in 1966.

"I believe managing is like holding a dove in your hand. If you hold it too tightly you kill it, but if you hold it too loosely, you lose it."

—Tommy Lasorda, baseball

"When I was coaching, the one thought that I would try to get across to my players was that everything I do each day, everything I say, I must first think what effect it will have on everyone concerned."

—Frank Layden, basketball

"We were looking for three qualities in our coach. First, he had to be a good teacher. He needed to be able to work well within the organization. He had to because he can't do it alone, and he had to have the respect of the players."

—Marv Levy, football

"Coaches who can outline plays on a blackboard are a dime a dozen. The ones who win get inside their players and motivate."

—Vince Lombardi, football

"Go with the best you've got."

—Al Lopez. baseball

"You have to convince your players that the only reason a play failed was that they didn't execute properly."

—Bill McCartney, football

"Learn to know every man under you, get under his skin, know his faults. Then cater to him—with kindness or roughness as his case may demand."

—John McGraw, baseball

"I want my teams to have my personality: surly, obnoxious, and arrogant."

—Al McGuire, basketball

"After all my years, there are two things I've never got used to—haggling with a player over his contract and telling a boy he's got to go back."

—Connie Mack, baseball

"We watch the good things you do so you can see how and why you did them. We watch the average things so you can improve on them, and we watch the bad things you do so you won't do them again."

—John Madden, football

"I'm not the manager because I'm always right, but I'm always right because I'm the manager."

—Gene Mauch, baseball

"A life of frustration is inevitable for any coach whose main enjoyment is winning."

—Chuck Noll, football

"A good coach will make his players see what they can be rather than what they are."

—Ara Parseghian, football

"In the end, I've found, people like the direct approach. It's much more valuable to them to have a leader who's absolutely clear and open than to have one who soft-soaps or talks in circles."

—Bill Parcells, football

"Coaches have the same obligation as all teachers at our institutions, except we probably have more influence over our young people than anyone other than their families. We're dealing with emotions, we're dealing with commitment—and loyalty, and pride: the things that make a difference in a person's life."

—Joe Paterno, football

"The only way to get people to like working hard is to motivate them. Today, people must understand why they're working hard. Every individual in an organization is motivated by something different."

—Rick Pitino, basketball

"Remember coaching is not a natural way of life. Your victories and losses are too clear cut."

—Tommy Prothro, football

"You can motivate by fear, and you can motivate by reward. But both those methods are only temporary. The only lasting thing is self-motivation."

—Homer Rice, football

"Look for your choices, pick the best one, then go with it."

—Pat Riley, basketball

"I'll never forget September 6, 1950. I got a letter threatening me, Hank Bauer, Yogi Berra, and Johnny Mize. It said if I showed up in uniform against the Red Sox I'd be shot. I turned the letter over to the FBI and told my manager Casey Stengel about it. You know what Casey did? He gave me a different uniform and gave mine to Billy Martin. Can you imagine that! Guess Casey thought it'd be better if Billy got shot."

—Phil Rizzuto, baseball

"Leadership, like coaching, is fighting for the hearts and souls of men and getting them to believe in you."

—Eddie Robinson, football

"I never criticize a player unless they are convinced of my unconditional confidence in them."

—John Robinson, football

"I have heard of managers who encourage players not to slide hard for fear they will get hurt and be lost from the lineup for a time. That is why you occasionally see a player go into second base on a double play ball and not even bother to slide. I wonder, could Ty Cobb sit through plays like that and hold his lunch."

—Frank Robinson, baseball

"A coach's greatest asset is his sense of responsibility—the reliance placed on him by his players. Handling our personnel is the most important phase of coaching. The secret of coaching success can be reduced to a simple formula: strict discipline in your training program and on the field, combined with a high and continuing interest in all your other relationships with your kids."

—Knute Rockne, football

"You know, a football coach is nothing more than a teacher. You teach them the same subject, and you have a group of new guys every year."

—Darrell Royal, football

"I believe that you're either with us or against us in reference to the team. Is the team with the management and coaching staff and will they do whatever it takes to be a winner? We're in it together. A house divided will not stand. Second, the only way an individual can ever achieve the ultimate success is to be a part of the team. The most difficult thing to teach is how do you get out of yourself and with the program to help the team. You have to want to be here, and you have to want to do it. Third, it will never make a difference what happens, win or lose. It's how you grow from it. It's how you deal with it. It's how you take it. That's our greatest challenge, not to run away from it. Finally, the only thing you can count on in life is change. When change rears its head, you have to adapt."

—Pat Riley, basketball

"I'm not a yeller. My theory is that no one goes out there trying to screw up."

—Amy Ruley, basketball

"I think what coaching is all about is taking players and analyzing their ability and putting them in a position where they can excel within the framework of the team winning."

—Don Shula, football

"You should sub a player out when you see a player not going full speed or playing selfish basketball."

—Dean Smith, basketball

"The secret to managing is to keep the guys who hate you away from the guys who are undecided."

—Casey Stengel, baseball

"I don't think a manager should be judged by whether he wins the pennant, but by whether he gets the most out of the twenty-five men he's been given."

—Chuck Tanner, baseball

"The more your players have to think on the court, the slower their feet get."

—Jerry Tarkanian, basketball

"I'm not into that business of being relevant to kids. I'm not playing on their team. They're playing on mine. We have certain ways of acting here. My kids are not going to come in here and say, 'Hey, baby.' It doesn't make you less of a man to have respect for people."

—John Thompson, basketball

"I've never managed to save my job. I have to manage to try to win. If I start thinking, 'If I do this, it'll look better than if I do that,' I can't do that. Even if you're going to get fired, you do the things you think you should do."

—Joe Torre, baseball

"You need to be as distinctive as you can. Rather than say, 'Throw it to him,' we would say, 'Throw it to the numbers' or 'Throw it to the outside of where the defender was.' You want to be as specific as you can, so then you have a reference point."

—Bill Walsh, football

"A manager should stay as far away as possible from his players."

—Earl Weaver, baseball

"I let them know that I believe that they can succeed, and I'm going to be there to help them."

—Lenny Wilkens, basketball

"Play against the game, not your opponent."

—Bud Wilkinson, football

BILL WALSH

Bill Walsh was born November 30, 1931, in Los Angeles. He attended college at San Jose State, where he was a star wide receiver. Following college he coached football at Washington High School in Fremont, California. He moved to the college level as an assistant coach at the University of California. He first coached in the pros in the old AFL as head coach of the Oakland Raiders in 1966. He was an assistant coach for the Cincinnati Bengals under Paul Brown for seven years beginning in 1968. He was an assistant coach for the San Diego Chargers in 1975. Returning to college, he became the head coach at Stanford from 1977–1978. His next job was the one for which he would become famous. From 1979 until 1988 he was the head coach of the San Francisco 49ers. While there he won three Super Bowls. He is credited with inventing the "West Coast offense" which replaces ground-control running plays with short precision passes, often to running backs coming out of the backfield. Fourteen of his assistant coaches went on to become NFL head coaches. After his tenure with the 49ers, Walsh returned to Stanford in 1993 and coached for one season. He was inducted into the Football Hall of Fame in 1993. Walsh died in 2007 at age 75 following a long battle with leukemia. Following his death, NFL commissioner Roger Goodell said, "His Hall of Fame coaching accomplishments speak for themselves, but the essence of Bill Walsh was that he was an extraordinary teacher. If you gave him a blackboard and a piece of chalk, he would become a whirlwind of wisdom. He taught all of us not only about football but also about life and how it takes teamwork for any of us to succeed as individuals."

"I think anyone in a position of supervision, if they're not listening to those under them, they're not going to get good results. The supervisor must make sure that all those under his supervision understand they're working with him, not for him. I think if you work for someone, you punch the clock in and out and that's it. If you're working with someone, you want to do more than that."

—John Wooden, basketball

SECURITY

"Security comes from earning it—not seeking it."

—Marv Levy, football

"Act like you expect to get into the end zone. Believe deep down inside that you are destined to do great things."

—Joe Paterno, football

SEIZING THE MOMENT

"In basketball—as in life—true joy comes from being fully present in each and every moment, not just when things are going your way. Of course, it's no accident that things are more likely to go your way when you stop worrying about whether you're going to win or lose and focus your full attention on what's happening right this moment."

—Phil Jackson, basketball

SELF-DISCIPLINE

"Without self-discipline, success is impossible, period."

—Lou Holtz, football

"More players lick themselves than are ever licked by an opposing team. The first thing any man has to know is how to handle himself."

—Connie Mack, baseball

"How to use your leisure time is the biggest problem of a ballplayer."

—Branch Rickey, baseball

"Discipline yourself, and others won't need to. If you lose self-control, everything will fail. You cannot function physically or mentally or in any other way unless your emotions are under control."

—John Wooden, basketball

SELF-IMPROVEMENT

"The principle is competing against yourself. It's about self-improvement, about being better than you were the day before."

—Steve Young, football

SELFLESSNESS

"The best way to forget one's self is to look at the world with attention and love."

—Red Auerbach, basketball

"To me, teamwork is the beauty of our sport, where you have five acting as one. You become selfless."

—Mike Krzyzewski, basketball

"You can't live a perfect day without doing something for someone who will never be able to repay you."

—John Wooden, basketball

SIMPLE BUT NOT EASY

"Our style is simple but not that easy. Roll up your sleeves and play good, solid football. We want to develop a quality football team that is going to last. Our goal is to win the Super Bowl and win it again and again. I try to promote philosophical ideas. The goal was to get them to be unselfish and rely on the other players. Winning didn't need to be the goal. Winning will come if you do the other things."

—Marv Levy, football

SOUL

"Don't ever forget that you play with your soul as well as your body."

—Kareem Abdul-Jabbar, basketball

"I gave it my body and mind, but I have kept my soul."

—Phil Jackson, basketball

SPIRIT

"The spirit, the will to win, and the will to excel are the things that endure. These qualities are so much more important than the events that occur."

—Vince Lombardi, football

"Training gives us an outlet for suppressed energies created by stress and thus tones the spirit just as exercise conditions the body."

—Arnold Schwarzennegger, bodybuilding

SPORTSMANSHIP

"Show me a good loser and I'll show you a loser."

—Red Auerbach, basketball

"The only way to prove you're a good sport is to lose."

—Ernie Banks, baseball

"Any pitcher who throws at a batter and deliberately tries to hit him is a communist.

—Alvin Dark, baseball

"Sportsmanship is not just about being nice. It is much more important than that. It's about realizing that you could not compete without an opponent and that she has the same goals as you."

—-Stephanie Deibler, softball, volleyball

"'How you play the game' is for college ball. When you're play-ing for money, winning is the only thing that matters. Win any way as long as you can get away with it. Nice guys finish last."

—Leo Durocher, baseball

"They say football is America's greatest game, but it's not. The greatest game in America is called opportunity. Football is merely a great expression of it."

—Joe Kapp, football

LEO DUROCHER

Leo Durocher's career came in two acts. In the first he was an all-glove, no-stick infielder who played twenty years in the major leagues for the Yankees, Reds, Cardinals, and Brooklyn Dodgers. Twice he played on pennant winners, in 1928 and 1934.

Act two came after his playing days were through and he made a quick transition to manager. He helmed one ball club or another for 22 of the next 34 years (1939–1973). He is best remembered as a fiery, do-anything-to-win style manager, who plagued umpires, scoffed at the rules, and proclaimed proudly, "Nice guys finish last."

He had a wild on-the-field demeanor, and all indications are that his life was wilder than most off the field as well. He was mar-ried from 1947–1960 to movie star Laraine Day and was suspended for a full season (1947) because of his involvement with gamblers.

Durocher was inducted to the Baseball Hall of Fame in 1994.

"I've tried to handle winning well, so that maybe we'll win again, but I've also tried to handle failure well. If those serve as good examples for teachers and kids, then I hope that would be a contribution I have made to sport. Not just basketball, but to sport."

—Mike Krzyzewski, basketball

"Whoever said 'It's not whether you win or lose that counts' probably lost."

—Martina Navratilova, tennis

"Tactics, fitness, stroke ability, adaptability, experience, and sportsmanship are all necessary for winning."

—Fred Perry, tennis

"One man practicing sportsmanship is far better than fifty preaching it."

—Knute Rockne, football

"On my tombstone just write, 'The sorest loser that ever lived.'"

—Earl Weaver, baseball

STATISTICS

"While statistics are interesting, they're all in the past."

—Vince Lombardi, football

STRATEGY

"It doesn't matter who scores the points, it's who can get the ball to the scorer."

—Larry Bird, basketball

"Are you crazy? An intentional walk with the bases empty? This is baseball, not backgammon!"

—Coach Buttermaker, baseball
(*Bad News Bears*, screenplay by Bill Lancaster)

"Let's be getting at them before they get at us."

—W. G. Grace, cricket

"Find out what the other team wants to do. Then take it away from them."

—George Halas, football

"There are really only two plays: *Romeo and Juliet*, and put the darn ball in the basket."

—Abe Lemons, basketball

"I just wrap my arms around the whole backfield and peel 'em one by one until I get to the ball carrier. Him I keep."

—Big Daddy Lipscomb, football

"Offensively, you do what you do best and do it again and again. Defensively, you attack your opponent's strength."

—Vince Lombardi, football

"Keep it simple; when you get too complex you forget the obvious."

—Al Maguire, basketball

"If we're going to run the football, and if we're going to be an explosive offense, it's going to start up there in the trenches."

—Steve Mariucci, football

"There are fifty games a year when you beat the crap out of them, and there's fifty games a year when they beat the crap out of you. The rest are swing games. You've got to win those if you are going to win."

—Tony Muser, baseball

"If a man can beat you, walk him."

—Leroy "Satchel" Paige, baseball

"The idea is not to block every shot. The idea is to make your opponent believe that you might block every shot."

—Bill Russell, basketball

"If you keep the opposition on their butts, they don't score goals."

—Fred Shero, hockey

"The key to winning baseball games is pitching, fundamentals, and three-run homers."

—Earl Weaver, baseball

STREET SMARTS

"I think everyone should go to college and get a degree and then spend six months as a bartender and six months as a cab-driver. Then they would really be educated."

—Al McGuire, basketball

STRESS

"You don't really know people until you get in the trenches with them, know how they think, know how they feel, know how they react."

—Frank Robinson, baseball

SUCCESS

"I think the biggest asset of successful people is that they are not afraid of success. There are so many people who are afraid of having success for fear of having to repeat their successful ways. It's so easy to see that in people. I'll read quotes in the newspaper, and I can tell people who are afraid to be good."

—Mike Bossy, hockey

"Sweat plus sacrifice equals success."

—Charlie Finley, baseball

"I think you've got to pay the price for anything that's worthwhile, and success is paying the price. You've got to pay the price to win, you've got to pay the price to stay on top, and you've got to pay the price to get there."

—Vince Lombardi, football

"Sports are 90 percent inspiration and 10 percent perspiration."

—Johnny Miller, golf

"Four years of football are calculated to breed in the average man more of the ingredients of success in life than almost any academic course he takes. I'll find out what my best team is when I find out how many doctors and lawyers and good husbands and good citizens have come off of each and every one of my teams."

—Knute Rockne, football

"Success is not the result of spontaneous combustion. You must first set yourself on fire."

—Fred Shero, hockey

SURRENDER

"The harder you work, the harder it is to surrender."

—Vince Lombardi, football

TAKING

"The strong take from the weak and the smart take from the strong."

—Pete Carril, basketball

TALENT

"Great football coaches have the vision to see, the faith to believe, the courage to do . . . and 25 great players."

—Marv Levy, football

"You can never have enough talent."

—Pat Riley, basketball

"The secret is to have eight great players and four others who will cheer like crazy."

—Jerry Tarkanian, basketball

"Talent is God-given. Be humble. Fame is man-given. Be grateful. Conceit is self-given. Be careful."

—John Wooden, basketball

TEACHERS

"How many people watch you give a final exam? Well, I have 50,000 watch me give mine—every Saturday!"

—Paul "Bear" Bryant, football

"When you want to win a game, you have to teach. When you lose a game, you have to learn."

—Tom Landry, football

"Styles of coaching may differ—from bombastic to philosophical. But at the end of the day, any good coach is a teacher."

—Marv Levy, football

"They call it coaching but it is teaching. You do not just tell them—you show them the reasons."

—Vince Lombardi, football

"The key to your success will not be what you do, but how well you teach what you do."

—John Robinson, football

"No written word, nor spoken plea
Can teach our children what they should be,
Nor all the books on all the shelves.
It's what the teachers are themselves."

—John Wooden, basketball

TEAM CONFIDENCE

"When a team outgrows individual performance and learns team confidence, excellence becomes a reality."

—Joe Paterno, football

TEAMWORK

"One man can be a crucial ingredient on a team, but one man cannot make a team."

—Kareem Abdul-Jabbar, basketball

"They said you have to use your five best players, but I found you win with the five who fit together the best."

—Red Auerbach, basketball

"There is an old saying about the strength of the wolf is the pack, and I think there is a lot of truth to that. On a football team, it's not the strength of the individual players, but it is the strength of the unit and how they all function together."

—Bill Belichick, football

"If you get the best players, you're going to get the kids who have egos. You have to take the 'I' concept out and get the 'we' concept."

—Bobby Bowden, football

"Nothing devastates a football team like a selfish player. It's a cancer."

—Paul Brown, football

"It's amazing how much can be accomplished if no one cares about who gets the credit."

—Blanton Collier, football

"We have to put the team ahead of our personal feelings."

—Terry Crisp, hockey

"Hard work and togetherness—they go hand in hand. You need the hard work because it's such a tough atmosphere . . . to win week in and week out. You need togetherness because you don't always win, and you gotta hang tough together."

—Tony Dungy, football

"Winning as a team is better than anything. It's great to share success."

—Jim Harbaugh, football

"On a good team there are no superstars. There are great players who show they are great players by being able to play with others as a team. They have the ability to be superstars, but if they fit into a good team, they make sacrifices, they do things necessary to help the team win. What the numbers are in salaries or statistics don't matter; how they play together does."

—Red Holzman, basketball

"Good teams become great ones when the members trust each other enough to surrender the Me for the We."

—Phil Jackson, basketball

"The strength of the team is each individual member; the strength of each member is the team."

—Dick Vitale, basketball

RED HOLZMAN

Red Holzman was a New Yorker through and through. He attended Franklin K. Lane High School in Jamaica, New York, in the borough of Queens. He played two years of basketball, was named to the All-Scholastic team in 1938, and has subsequently been enshrined in the PSAL Hall of Fame. After a stint at the University of Baltimore, he transferred to City College of New York where he was a hoops star. He played two years in the upper Manhattan school (1940–1942). He was both All-Metropolitan and All-American both of those years. In 1958 Red was enshrined in the CCNY Hall of Fame. World War II got in the way and Red served in the U.S. Navy from 1942–1945.

He got his first job as a pro basketball player as soon as the war was over, playing for the Rochester Royals of the old National Basketball League. He made the NBL All-Pro Team from 1945–1950. Three times he made the NBL All-Star Team. He played on the NBL championship team in 1946, and on an NBA championship team in 1951 (Rochester having moved to the NBA in the merger of the BAA and NBL). He stayed with the Royals until 1953.

He got his first experience coaching in the NBA as coach for the Milwaukee/St. Louis Hawks in 1953–1957. From 1957–1967 he was an assistant coach with the Knicks, then became the team's head coach from 1967–1982. By that time he was, and may forever be, the Knicks all-time greatest coach. He was coach for both of the franchise's two NBA championship campaigns in 1970 and 1973, and his 613 victories as head coach are by far the most of any coach. His overall record as Knicks coach was 613-384. His postseason record as a coach was 58-48. He was named the NBA Coach of the Year in 1970, and led the Knicks to the NBA finals in 1972. He was named the NBA Coach of the Decade for the 1970s. By winning with the Knicks in 1970, Red became one of only ten NBA players to win a championship both as a player and a coach.

About Red, Willis Reed once said, "Red tries to give one the impression that he's a hard, rough, impersonal coach. He's really just a pussycat with more knowledge of basketball than any man I've ever known." Red was the first recipient of the National Basketball Coaches Association Achievement Award in 1981 and became the author of four books. He was elected to the Basketball Hall of Fame in 1985, and continued with the Knicks as a consultant right up until he died of leukemia in 1998. His wife was Selma.

"Ask not what your teammates can do for you. Ask what you can do for your teammates."

—Earvin "Magic" Johnson, basketball

"There are plenty of teams in every sport that have great players and never win titles. Most of the time, those players aren't willing to sacrifice for the greater good of the team. The funny thing is, in the end, their unwillingness to sacrifice only makes individual goals more difficult to achieve. One thing I believe to the fullest is that if you think and achieve as a team, the individual accolades will take care of themselves. Talent wins games, but teamwork and intelligence win championships."

—Michael Jordan, basketball

"You develop a team to achieve what one person cannot accomplish alone. All of us alone are weaker, by far, than if all of us are together. . . . Two are better than one if two act as one."

—Mike Krzyzewski, basketball

"Teamwork is the ability to have different thoughts about things. It's the ability to argue and stand up and say loud and strong what you feel. But in the end, it's also the ability to adjust to what is the best for the team."

—Tom Landry, football

"It takes more that just a great coach or a great quarterback or a great anything. It takes the whole package."

—Marv Levy, football

"The achievements of an organization are the results of the combined effort of each individual. . . . Individual commitment to a group effort—that is what makes a team work, a company work, a society work, a civilization work."

—Vince Lombardi, football

"There's nothing greater in the world than when somebody on the team does something good, and everybody gathers around to pat him on the back."

—Billy Martin, baseball

"It is the name on the front of the jersey that matters most, not the one on the back."

—Joe Paterno, football

"Sometimes a player's greatest challenge is coming to grips with his role on the team."

—Scottie Pippen, basketball

"Individual glory is insignificant when compared to achieving victory as a team."

—Dot Richardson, softball

"Being a part of success is more important than being personally indispensable."

—Pat Riley, basketball

"The secret is to work less as individuals and more as a team. As a coach, I play not my eleven best, but my best eleven."

—Knute Rockne, football

PAT RILEY

Pat Riley attended Linton High School in Schenectady, New York, and played his college basketball at Kentucky under Adolph Rupp. He played in the 1966 NCAA national championship game, a game immortalized in the 2006 film *Glory Road*. Riley was an NBA rookie in 1967 for San Diego. He played three years in San Diego, then six years with the Lakers, before finishing his playing career in 1976 in Phoenix.

Riley came by his coaching ability honestly. His father was a high-school baseball coach and a minor-league baseball manager. Since his playing days Pat has won more than 1,000 games and four championships as an NBA head coach. Those championships came in 1982, 1985, 1987, and 1988 with the Lakers—the team that featured Kareem Abdul-Jabbar and Magic Johnson.

After coaching the Lakers from 1981–1990, he became the Knicks head coach from 1991–1995. The Knicks played great during the Riley era. His won-loss record was 223-105 regular season and 35-28 postseason. Although he took some time off, he has been head coach of the Miami Heat, for the most part, ever since.

As coach of the Lakers and then the Knicks, Riley was known to the casual fan as much for his Armani suits, chiseled jaw, and slicked-back hair as he was for his coaching style. Hardcore fans, on the other hand, realized that this was a man whose philosophy led to victory.

"The way a team plays as a whole determines its success. You may have the greatest bunch of individual stars in the world, but if they don't play together, the club won't be worth a dime."

—Babe Ruth, baseball

"You are not going to win with the kids who are just All-Americans. The kids must have more than status; they must have togetherness."

—John Thompson, basketball

"That's what it's all about. You need 25 guys to contribute."

—Joe Torre, baseball

"The glory of sport is witnessing a well-coached team perform as a single unit, striving for a common goal and ultimately bringing distinction to the jersey the players represent."

—Dick Vitale, basketball

"Winning is about having the whole team on the same page."

—Bill Walton, basketball

JOE TORRE

Although Joe Torre is best known as the manager of the New York Yankees, he had a long playing and managing career before he ever put on the pinstripes. Torre played from 1960 until 1977, and during that time hit 252 home runs and knocked in 1,185 RBI.

He began his career with the Milwaukee/Atlanta Braves as a teammate of Hank Aaron and finished with the New York Mets as a player/manager. In between he also played five seasons with the St. Louis Cardinals. He was voted the National League's Most Valuable Player in 1971, and played in nine All Star games.

Torre managed the Mets from 1977–1981, the Braves from 1982–1984, and the Cardinals from 1990–1995. He became Yankee manager in 1996 and won four World Championships in the Big Apple. He was twice named the American League's Manager of the Year in 1996 and 1998.

Torre was born in 1940 in Brooklyn, New York. His older brother Frank was also a major league ballplayer. Joe is the only person to amass more than 2,000 hits in his career and win more than 2,000 games as a manager. He is ninth on the all-time list for managerial victories.

Torre is candid about his childhood experiences as a witness to domestic violence and, along with his wife Ali, founded the Joe Torre Safe at Home Foundation which operates domestic violence resource centers.

"Success is peace of mind that is the direct result of self-satisfaction in knowing you did your best to become the best that you are capable of becoming."

—John Wooden, basketball

TEMPERAMENT

"Most football players are temperamental. That's 90 percent temper and 10 percent mental."

—Doug Plank, football

THINKING

"Football can be an intellectual exercise and I want people who will think about what we can do and not be content to rubber-stamp my thoughts or be satisfied with what has worked in the past."

—Joe Paterno, football

THREE QUESTIONS

"The answer to three questions will determine your success or failure. One, can people trust me to do my best? Two, am I committed to the task at hand? Three, do I care about other people and show it? If the answers to all three questions is yes, there is no way you can fail."

—Lou Holtz, football

TIES

"A tie is like kissing your sister."

—Paul "Bear" Bryant, football

TIME

"I don't sit there and watch the clock. That's what's great about baseball. There's no time limit. You can be 25,000 runs behind, but you can keep hitting."

—Johnny Oates, baseball

"You can't sit on a lead and run a few plays into the line and just kill the clock. You've got to throw the ball over the damn plate and give the other man his chance. That's why baseball is the greatest game of all."

—Earl Weaver, baseball

TOO MUCH INFO DEPT.

"Don't tell your problems to people: 80 percent don't care, and the other 20 percent are glad you have them."

—Lou Holtz, football

TOUGH SCHEDULES

"It is better to be devoured by lions than to be eaten by dogs."

—Alex Agase, football

TRUST

"He who believes in nobody knows that he himself is not to be trusted."

—Red Auerbach, basketball

"I think fans felt comfortable with us because they could trust us. They could trust how we played the game and conducted ourselves—especially in this era of negativity. Hopefully they feel like we did it the right way."

—Tony Gwynn, baseball (referring to himself and Cal Ripken, Jr., with whom he was being inducted into the Baseball Hall of Fame in 2007)

TRUTH

"I don't want a team that escapes from reality and escapes from the truth. I don't want people who are always escaping, who always have a story and are always conniving. An ostrich tries to escape from the truth. Isn't an ostrich the thing that puts its head in the sand? But guess what's sticking out when he does it? It's ass, that's what. I don't want a team like that. . . . Because when you have a team like that and trouble comes, that team will not face the trouble."

—John Chaney, basketball

UNDERDOGS

"Nobody roots for Goliath."

—Wilt Chamberlain, basketball

VALUES

"My family is more important than football, and my religion is more important than either one."

—Bobby Bowden, football

"The values learned on the playing field—how to set goals, endure, take criticism and risks, become team players, use our bodies, stay healthy and deal with stress—prepare us for life."

—Donna de Varona, swimming

VARIETY

"I use my single windup, my double windup, my triple windup, my hesitation windup, my no windup. I also use my step-n-pitch-it, my submariner, my sidearmer, and my bat dodger. Man's got to do what he's got to do."

—Leroy "Satchel" Paige, baseball

WAR

"Basketball is like war in that offensive weapons are developed first, and it always takes a while for the defense to catch up."

—Red Auerbach, basketball

"Pro football is like nuclear warfare. There are no winners, only survivors."

—Frank Gifford, football

WEAKNESSES

"Always turn a negative situation into a positive situation. My attitude is that if you push me towards something that you think is a weakness, then I will turn that perceived weakness into a strength."

—Michael Jordan, basketball

"Build up your weaknesses until they become your strong points."

—Knute Rockne, football

WILL

"The difference between a successful person and others is not a lack of strength, not a lack of knowledge, but rather a lack of will."

—Vince Lombardi, football

WINNERS

"A winner has dedication and pride and the will to win, and he'll do a little bit extra every day to improve himself and his team. A winner is worried about his team and his school, and he'll outwork people, and he'll sacrifice."

—Paul "Bear" Bryant, football

"A winner is someone who recognizes his God-given talents, works his tail off to develop them into skills, and uses these skills to accomplish his goals."

—Larry Bird, basketball

"First become a winner in life. Then it's easier to become a winner on the field."

—Tom Landry, football

"If you don't think you're a winner, you don't belong here."

—Vince Lombardi, football

WINNING

"From the word go, we're going to try and hit them as hard as we can."

—David Beckham, soccer

"Winning is the epitome of honesty itself."

—Woody Hayes, football

"If winning isn't everything, why do they keep score?"

—Vince Lombardi, football

"Everything looks nicer when you win. The girls are prettier. The cigars taste better. The trees are greener."

—Billy Martin, baseball

"When we lost I couldn't sleep at night. When we win I can't sleep at night. But when you win, you wake up feeling better."

—Joe Torre, baseball

WISDOM

"Wisdom is always an overmatch for strength."

—Phil Jackson, basketball

"You can tell by looking at me that I've got more miles behind me than I've got in front of me. When you reach that point, if you've got some good years left, you want to make sure that you use them wisely."

—Tom Osborne, football

WORK

"No one has ever drowned in sweat."

—Lou Holtz, football

"All right Mister, let me tell you what winning means . . . you're willing to go longer, work harder, give more than anyone else."

—Vince Lombardi, football

WORKING TOGETHER

"People who work together will win, whether it be against complex football defenses, or the problems of modern society."

—Vince Lombardi, football

WORRYING

"When you're the manager of a team, all the worries of the team become your worries."

—Al Lopez, baseball

"I worry about the things I can affect, and the things I have no control over I move by."

—Lenny Wilkens, basketball

PHIL JACKSON

Phil Jackson was chosen by New York in the second round of the NBA draft, the 17th overall pick. He spent ten full seasons as a Knick, almost never starting. He served as the back-up center for Willis Reed and then for Jerry Lucas. Jackson began his Knicks career in 1967–1968 and was named to the NBA's All-Rookie team for his precocious efforts. Unfortunately he missed the Knicks championship year, 1969–1970, because of a back injury, but he was around for their second championship in 1973. During that first championship season he kept busy by writing a book along with Knicks team photographer George Kalinsky. The book was called *Take it All!* It was a photo-essay book and was heralded upon its release as a new literary form. Phil was always effective on the court. He had a hook shot, and his long arms made him a bothersome defensive force. But he was no ball handler. People got so nervous when Phil put the ball on the floor that Coach Holzman put him on a "two-dribble limit." Kalinsky once wrote that Phil Jackson dribbling resembled Groucho Marx "crawl-walking." During the two seasons he played the most, 1973–1975, he averaged about eleven points per game, and in the second of those seasons he led the NBA in personal fouls. He also played in the postseason for the Knicks eight times, for a total of 67 games, scoring 7.7 points per game. He left the Knicks on June 8, 1978, in a trade with the New Jersey Nets, accompanying an exchange of future draft choices. As a Net he played little and filled a player/assistant coach role. He retired as an active player in 1980.

Phil grew up in Montana and North Dakota, the son of a fundamentalist preacher from the Assembly of God Pentecostal church. For his first two years at the University of North Dakota Phil played both basketball and baseball. He was scouted by the Los Angeles Dodgers after his sophomore year but decided at that point to quit baseball and to concentrate all of his attention on basketball, a move that paid off for him.

After retiring as a player, Phil took a year off before taking a job as a TV commentator on Nets broadcasts. He spent five seasons coaching the Albany Patroons of the CBA, once leading the team to the league championship and once earning the CBA's Coach of the Year award. In 1987 he became assistant coach for the Chicago Bulls. After a couple of seasons Phil was promoted to the head coaching job. From 1989 to the present, with some time off a few years back to recharge his batteries, Phil Jackson has been a successful NBA coach. He won nine NBA championships as coach of the Bulls and the Lakers, although he would be the first to admit that having Michael Jordan and Scottie Pippin in Chicago and Shaq and Kobe in L.A. helped a lot. Counting his championship with the Knicks, Jackson has as many rings as he has fingers. He is tied with Red Auerbach for most NBA championships while coaching. Phil is famous for putting Eastern wisdom into his coaching sermons, which has earned him the nickname "The Zen Master."

YOUTH

"Professional coaches measure success in rings. College coaches measure success in championships. High school coaches measure success in titles. Youth coaches measure success in smiles."

—Paul McAllister, basketball

ZEN

"Like life, basketball is messy and unpredictable. It has its way with you, no matter how hard you try to control it. The trick is to experience each moment with a clear mind and open heart. When you do that, the game—and life—will take care of itself. . . . If you meet the Buddha in the lane, feed him the ball."

—Phil Jackson, basketball